IN A MINOR KEY

Negro Youth in Story and Fact

MEMBERS OF THE AMERICAN YOUTH COMMISSION

Appointed by the American Council on Education

WILL W. ALEXANDER, Washington

CLARENCE A. DYKSTRA, Madison

DOROTHY CANFIELD FISHER, Arlington, Vermont

WILLARD E. GIVENS, Washington

HENRY I. HARRIMAN, Boston

GEORGE JOHNSON, Washington

MORDECAI W. JOHNSON, Washington

CHESTER H. ROWELL, San Francisco

WILLIAM F. RUSSELL, New York

JOHN W. STUDEBAKER, Washington

HENRY C. TAYLOR, Chicago

MIRIAM VAN WATERS, Framingham, Massachusetts

MATTHEW WOLL, New York

ROBERT E. WOOD, Chicago

OWEN D. YOUNG, New York

GEORGE F. ZOOK, *ex officio*, Washington

———

FLOYD W. REEVES, *Director*

IN A MINOR KEY

Negro Youth in Story and Fact

BY IRA DeA. REID

Prepared for

The American Youth Commission

GREENWOOD PRESS, PUBLISHERS
WESTPORT, CONNECTICUT

FOREWORD

THE DISADVANTAGES that have been attached to the condition of being a Negro in the United States have made it inevitable that the interests of Negro people should figure prominently in any inquiry into American social and economic problems. Realizing this fact early in its history, the American Youth Commission decided that it would be necessary to make extensive special studies of the conditions and needs of Negro youth.

This preliminary volume brings together much of the general information now available about Negro youth in this country. It will be followed by a number of research studies designed to penetrate further into the significance of what it means to be born a member of America's largest racial minority. The volumes in this series are:

> *Children of Bondage: The Personality Development of Negro Youth in the Urban South.* Allison Davis and John Dollard.
>
> *Negro Youth at the Crossways: Their Personality Development in the Middle States.* E. Franklin Frazier.
>
> *Growing Up in the Black Belt: Negro Youth in the Rural South.* Charles S. Johnson.
>
> *Color and Human Nature: Negro Personality Development in a Northern City.* W. Lloyd Warner, Buford H. Junker, and Walter A. Adams.

These studies of Negro youth were begun under the Commission's former director, Homer P. Rainey, now president of the University of Texas. In the initial planning of them, Dr. Rainey was assisted by Robert L. Sutherland, professor of sociology in

Bucknell University, who later served as associate director of the Commission in charge of studies of Negro youth. A summary of the findings of the entire project, together with a program of recommendations for educational and social planning, is being prepared by Dr. Sutherland for publication under the tentative title, *Color, Class, and Personality*.

The American Youth Commission was established in 1935 by the American Council on Education from which it received a mandate to:

1. consider all the needs of youth and appraise the facilities and resources for serving those needs;

2. plan experiments and programs which will be most helpful in solving the problems of youth;

3. popularize and promote desirable plans of action through publications, conferences, and demonstrations.

As in the case of other staff reports prepared for the Commission, the author of the present volume is responsible for the statements which are made; they are not necessarily endorsed by the Commission or by its Director. The Director does take responsibility for the organization of all research projects, the selection of staff, and the approval of staff reports as meriting publication. The Commission is responsible for the determination of the general areas in which research is conducted under its auspices, and from time to time it adopts and publishes statements which represent specifically the conclusions and recommendations of the Commission.

FLOYD W. REEVES
Director

March 1, 1940

PREFACE

A NEW RACE is growing up in America. Its skin is brown. In its veins is the blood of the three principal branches of man— black, white, yellow-brown. The new race numbers twelve million in the United States, and other millions in the West Indies and Central America. The group is new in its biological make-up; in its culture it is almost entirely cut off from the ancient African home. . . . But in reality the new race is not simply a percentage of the American population. It is distinctive. It still represents liabilities to the nation; it still suffers great hurts from the neighboring races; but it also contributes its own gifts."

How do the youth of this new socio-racial group, as pictured by Embree in *Brown America,* fare in their conditions of daily living? How healthy are they; how well organized their leisure time; and how frequent their visits to jail? In what kind of houses do they live? How long do they continue in school? What nature of work or relief do they find? By answering these questions and giving other significant statistics this volume tells the story of the modern Negro in a manner that should stimulate the thought of all who are concerned about the future of American youth. The lay reader will find *In a Minor Key* an interesting condensation of important facts. The educator, social worker, and student of minority groups will see in it a convenient reference source when brief summaries are needed.

Because of his experience in the fields of research, social work, and education, Ira DeA. Reid, professor of sociology at Atlanta University, was invited to prepare this book. Educated at Morehouse College, the University of Pittsburgh, and Columbia University, Mr.

Reid had served as a staff member of the National Urban League for nearly ten years before taking up his work at Atlanta, and had been responsible for a number of important studies sponsored by the League and by other agencies. He conducted extensive surveys of the Negro population in New Jersey communities and in the city of Baltimore. Among his more recent publications are: *A Study of Immigration in the United States, 1899–1937*, and *The Urban Negro Worker in the United States, 1925–1936*. Mr. Reid directed the latter study for the United States Department of the Interior in co-operation with the Works Progress Administration.

In assembling material for the present volume, Mr. Reid sifted from the general studies of Negro life those facts which pertain especially to Negro youth. He drew heavily upon government publications and also examined a large number of unpublished dissertations. *In a Minor Key* includes data assembled and summarized from all of these sources and presents them in a form easily accessible to anyone interested in the status of Negro youth.

ROBERT L. SUTHERLAND
Associate Director for Studies of Negro Youth

AUTHOR'S ACKNOWLEDGMENTS

ACKNOWLEDGMENT is made to Lincoln University for permission to quote Langston Hughes' "Youth," to the Viking Press for permission to quote from Edwin R. Embree's *Brown America,* and to the Friendship Press for permission to quote from Charles S. Johnson's *A Preface to Racial Understanding.*

Acknowledgment is also made to: Forrest E. Keller of the West Virginia University; Philip L. Harriman of Bucknell University; and M. M. Chambers, D. L. Harley, and A. C. Rosander of the American Youth Commission for their careful reading and criticism of the manuscript.

IRA DEA. REID

CONTENTS

CHARTS

YOUTH

We have tomorrow
Bright before us
Like a flame

Yesterday
A night-gone thing
A sun-down name

And dawn—today
Broad arch above the road
         we came
We march.

        —Langston Hughes

I. TO BEGIN WITH

The Introduction

TO BEGIN WITH

THE STORY

NEGRO YOUTH! Wasn't it a character in Goldsmith's *Citizen of the World* who, when asked to write an essay on Chinese Metaphysics, went to the encyclopedia, read the article on China, then the one on Metaphysics, put the two together, and called the product Chinese Metaphysics? Some such methodology could be employed in a discussion of Negro youth, but its value would be limited, for in this field of social living the laws of mathematics yield not two, but three, when one and one are added. The mere combination of "Negro" and "youth" yields not a union of factors that are racial and situations that are youthful, but a new combination that is possessed of the sound and fury of both terms with a meaning and significance all its own.

Negro youth cannot be identified entirely by use of genealogical tables, nor can its problems and its environment be completely measured by statistics. Being a Negro in the United States is sometimes an estate of which one can be justly proud; at other times it is a thing apart from all that is good and desirable in a democratic society. In many of its phases Negro youth is a group that exists in a world separate from American youth's common experiences. But why has this come to be so? Why are books written about the colored minority as a group set apart from other youth?

The answer begins to emerge at the very beginning of their story. Because of inadequate care, their mothers are more apt to die in childbirth than are those of other racial groups. When to Negro youth school age comes around, more than half of them attend the poorest schools in our country. When they must go to work, a smaller proportion of their number enjoys the opportunity to achieve high places or to acquire comfortable middle-class incomes for their services; most of them have to struggle at the lowest level of our economic life. They marry at an earlier age than white youth, rear families and settle down to a circumscribed existence within the traditional order of race and culture.

Like other youth, they start out with ambitions, hopes, and the willingness to go on and on in their pursuit of "success." Like other youth they face frustrations, defeats, and reprisals. Like other American youth, they have not riotously rebelled. They have been slow to form an aggressive youth movement. But, more so than other youth, their way of life is roughened and obstructed, from birth to death, by the factor of race. Race may not dominate but at least it throws its shadow across every phase of the Negro youth's life in the North and envelops every aspect of it in the South. From birth to death his is not only an outer environment of social and economic problems and adjustments, but also an inner environment of being Negro—which in the United States is interpreted to mean inferior, impoverished, and inconvenienced. Both of these environments are real, effective, and inescapable. They not only determine the status of Negroes but they also create the Negro personality—a personality that has had to develop in whatever way and to whatever extent it could within the iron ring of race prejudice. Like the simplest plant, the Negro youth has developed protective devices for survival and has been shaped by the environments that have nurtured him.

Today—while perhaps it could hardly be thought surprising if the opposite were true—the challenging fact of the matter is that Negro youth seem more "alive" than ever before. Their hopes, their ambitions, and their high resolves dramatize the contrast between the "what-is" of the present and the "what-may-be" of tomorrow.

4

THEIR NUMBERS ARE INCREASING

The Growth of the Negro Population

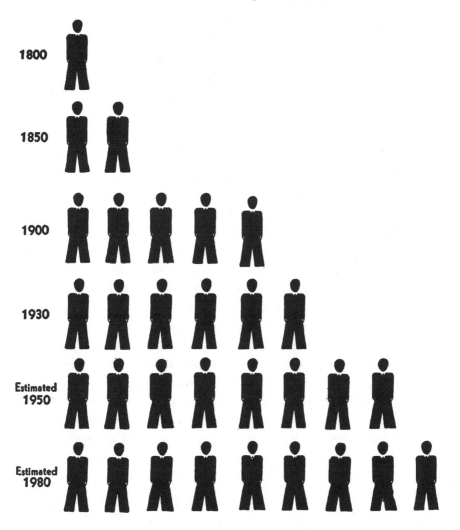

Each symbol represents two million Negroes

The "what-is" of today indicates that there are two theoretically perfect solutions to the adjustment of the Negro population in the United States. One is its complete isolation; the other its absolute fusion into the culture and racial body of the white population. The first solution we might dismiss as being no longer possible; the second, though proposed by an occasional idealist who is seeking a Utopia in race relations, is at present remotely far from realization. Between these two extremes of complete adjustment stands reality, exemplified in the divergent trends of the Negro community. Therein are expressed both the theory and the practice of isolation and fusion. Therein is found an accommodation of these two forces, but only a temporary and a partial accommodation, for new problems of adjustment are constantly arising. The Negro community, therefore, stands out as a permanent zone of social and physical transition, a zone of partial adjustment and of recurring conflict.

Negro communities throughout the United States possess certain features that serve as a common bond of identification. The mere separation of the races by residence and the presence of substandard conveniences in the colored areas reflect their ghetto-like aspect. To the New York Negro, "going to Harlem" may mean "going home." To the pleasure-bent or curiosity-seeking white New Yorker, "going to Harlem" usually means "going slumming." So far it has been impossible in the United States to separate races and maintain equality of status, convenience, and social participation. In cities and towns of the North as well as of the South, examples of inequalities in income, housing, health, sanitation, education, and protection of the Negro community as compared with other areas are faced daily. Through these inequalities there is expressed in the structure of each community a recognition of the race factor, and the Negro district becomes an area of race-feeling, race-thinking, and race-acting. It becomes an area where the Negro grows more aware of himself and of others and builds up the complex structure of intraracial and extraracial associations that permeate many aspects of his life.

Negro communities though possessing these similarities do, of course, differ on the bases of (*a*) the degree of interracial adjustment, (*b*) the quality and quantity of the socio-economic determinants, and (*c*) the force of intraracial factors. For most of his American sojourn the Negro has been a rural dweller. Today finds him an integral part of life in the "Great Cities," the "Middletowns," and the "Littletowns," while in the rural areas resides a smaller proportion of his race than ever before, though still a majority.

In matters of adjustment between the races these Negro communities vary. In the New England, Middle Atlantic, and North Central states they are more likely to be *areas of relative freedom,* where the Negro enjoys most of the political and some of the social rights of the general population. Such border states as West Virginia, Maryland, Kentucky, and Delaware are *areas of restricted social participation,* where the political rights of the Negro are observed, but where segregate social practices in public places call attention to the Negro's separateness. The South Atlantic and East South Central states contain communities of more complete subordination of the Negro. Here he is the permanent pariah, always given something apart and never sharing fully and equally in the political, economic, and social life. Then there are the several all-Negro villages, *areas of racial isolation,* where almost complete separation has resulted in a minimum amount of friction. Finally, there are those areas of the North, West, and East where Negroes in small numbers have lived for a long period of time and have known relatively little difference in their status as individuals and citizens from that of their white neighbors; but seldom can even these communities be called *areas of complete participation.*

According to their economic function the Negro communities which reflect the superordinate–subordinate relations of whites and Negroes most typically are those localities in which a majority of Negro workers are engaged in service or labor occupations for the white community. In the industrial centers of Birmingham, Pittsburgh, Chicago, Detroit, Steelton, and Gary, on the other hand, there is added to the service occupations some opportunity for industrial employment although types of work and advancement are limited by caste restrictions. In a special class are the smaller communities like Hampton, Lincoln, and Talladega and the larger centers like Nashville, New Orleans, and Atlanta where the Negro has been specially favored by outside philanthropy or public funds in the establishment of educational, health, and social agencies. Although such institutions have had an important effect upon the cultural life of the Negro community and upon interrace relations, they have also been significant economically in that they provide types of middle- and upper-class employment that would otherwise not be available.

There are important variations within the Negro community itself, but the usual classification of upper, middle, and lower class, based largely on the ownership of economic goods, does not completely interpret the Negro community's structure, because of the fact that Negroes own almost none of the basic instruments of production, control relatively little land, have few persons of great wealth, and are excluded from many of the positions of prestige occupied by whites. Because of these limitations, the members of the Negro community are, on a strictly economic basis, assigned with few exceptions to the lower and lower-middle classes of a stratified society. If, however, the class structure is considered more broadly in terms of functional association, we find that the Negro communities, like the white, have a well-organized hierarchy of relationships. Admission to the more exclusive upper circles is determined to some extent by economic success but also by family tradition, education, place of residence, degree of Negroidness, and a complex of other factors.

But, for the time being, the theories and subtleties of social relationships in the Negro community—though matters of profound importance—must await the results of the research studies mentioned in the Preface. Our task in the chapters that are to follow is limited to the story and the fact of those stark realities which are close at hand and are more easily observable.

8

GOING TO TOWN
The Story of Urbanization and the Negro

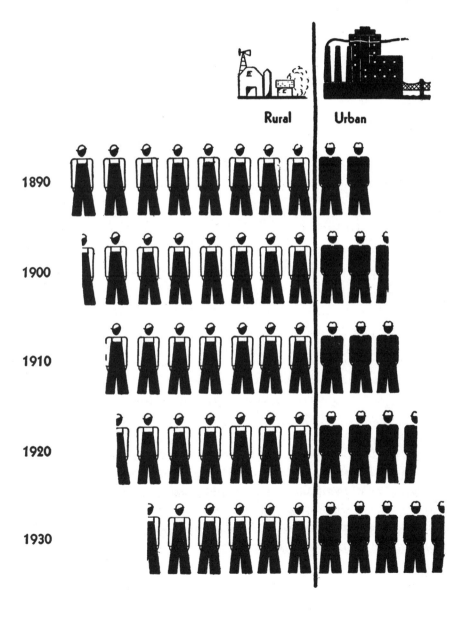

Rural   Urban

1890

1900

1910

1920

1930

Each symbol represents 10 per cent of the Negro population

THE FACT

1. On the average, among any thousand youth in the United States between 16 and 24 years of age about 105 Negroes will be found. In Maine there will be only one Negro youth in every thousand; in Mississippi, about 520 in every thousand. Eleven per cent, or more than 2,200,000 of all youth in the United States, were identified by the 1930 census as Negro. In the South, however, 26.5 per cent of all youth were Negro. In the northern states east of Colorado and Montana, 3.4 per cent were Negro, and in the western states only 0.9 per cent were Negro.

2. Negroes—black, brown, yellow, and white—in the United States in 1930 numbered nearly 12,000,000. This is somewhat less than double the number of such persons enumerated in 1880, over five times the number in 1830, and nearly 16 times the total number of Negroes at the time of the first enumeration in 1790.

3. It is estimated by the National Resources Committee that by 1980, when the United States is expected to reach its largest population, Negroes will number 18,000,000 and will form approximately 12 per cent of the total. The 2,454,000 Negro youth between the ages of 15 and 24 in the United States in 1930 are expected to increase to 2,666,000 in 1950, and to reach a peak of 2,786,000 in 1980.

4. Estimates of the Scripps Foundation indicate that in 1940 in 13 southern states there are approximately 36,000,000 persons, slightly less than 25 per cent of whom are Negroes.

5. At the outbreak of the Civil War 92 per cent of the Negro population of the United States was living south of the Mason-Dixon line. In 1930 about 20 per cent of the total Negro population was living north of this line. Unlike the white population, however, relatively few Negroes have gone to the Far West.

6. In 1930 there were 19 counties in the United States where Negroes formed more than 75 per cent of the population. These counties were distributed as follows: Mississippi, 8; Alabama, 6; Georgia, 2; Arkansas, Louisiana, and Virginia, 1 each. In Lowndes County, Alabama, and in Tunica County, Mississippi, there are six Negroes to every white person. More than 56 per cent of the Negroes living in the North and West in 1930 were born in the South. Less than 1 per cent of the southern Negro population was born in other sections.

7. The northward migration of Negroes has been almost entirely to large urban centers. In 1930, 88 per cent of the Negro population of the North and 32 per cent of all southern Negroes lived in cities.

8. Negroes in urban areas increased 251 per cent between 1890 and 1930, while in rural areas during the same period they increased 12 per cent.

9. The northern Negroes are not only an urbanized population but they are living for the most part in the large cities. Nearly one-half of the Negroes in the states north of the Mason-Dixon line are concentrated in nine cities with total populations of 100,000 or more inhabitants. There were 80 cities in the United States in 1930 with a Negro population of 10,000 or more. In general, the proportion of Negroes in the total population is increasing in the northern cities.

10. The age distribution of the Negro population has been affected by the cityward migration. This movement involves chiefly persons in the middle years of life; members of both the younger and the older age groups remain behind. Consequently, the proportion of persons in the productive years of life is greater in the urban population than in the rural. At the 1930 enumeration 38 per cent of the urban and 23 per cent of the rural Negroes were within the ages 25 to 44. In the rural areas 29 per cent of the Negroes in

villages and 21 per cent of those on farms were in the same age group.

11. In 1930 children under five years of age amounted to about 9 per cent of the white population and 10 per cent of the Negro population.

12. Between 1880 and 1930 the percentages of Negroes in age groups under 20 have decreased while those above 20 have increased.

13. Among Negroes there is an excess of females relative to males in all age groups under 45 years. The excess of females in this age range is greatest in years of early maturity—15 to 35 years. In 1930, the excess of females was greatest in the 20- to 24-year-group, where there were eight females to every seven males.

II. LIFE AND DEATH

Children are born . . . some grow older . . . the group gets thinner in the middle . . . a few continue a kind of hobbling march . . .

LIFE AND DEATH

THE STORY

LIFE COMES frequently to the Negro population; death comes both soon and late. Do you recall Addison's picture of the life span in the "Vision of Mirza"? It bears repeating here:

The bridge thou seest, said he, is human life; consider it attentively. Upon a more leisurely survey of it, I found that it consisted of three-score and ten entire arches, with several broken arches which added to those that were entire, made up the number about an hundred. As I was counting the arches the genius told me that this bridge consisted at first of a thousand arches; but that a great flood swept away the rest, and left the bridge in the ruinous condition I now beheld it. But tell me further, said he, what thou discoverest on it. I see multitudes of people passing over it, said I, and a black cloud hanging on each end of it. As I looked more attentively, I saw several of the passengers dropping through the bridge into the great tide that flowed underneath it; and upon further examination perceived there were innumerable trap-doors that lay concealed in the bridge, which the passengers no sooner trod upon, but they fell through them into the tide and immediately disappeared. These hidden pit-falls were set very thick at the entrance to the bridge, so that throngs of people no sooner broke through the cloud, but many of them fell into them. They grew thinner towards the middle, but multiplied and lay closer together towards the end of the arches that were entire.

There were indeed some persons, but their number was very small, that continued a kind of hobbling march on the broken arches, but fell through one after another, being quite tired and spent with so long a walk.

15

The mere facts of physical life and death create some of Negro youth's more serious problems. Their education, economic efficiency, and vitality are all affected. The racial population which embraces Negro youth has a higher birth rate, a higher sickness rate, and a higher death rate than found among the white population in the United States. Physical examinations for all school children, and especially for Negro children in the South, are few, and many of them are so perfunctory as to be of little worth. Facilities for treating their afflictions, if present, are almost certain to be inadequate. Tuberculosis continues to rage among Negro youth 15 to 19 years of age, with a mortality seven times as high as that among white youth of the same ages. Deaths from food poisoning are more numerous. Medical services available to them are inadequate and costly. So it seems almost a miracle that so many Negro youth do pass the teens and enter manhood and womanhood.

The most recent evidence indicates that the high mortality rates of the colored population are in excess of the white rates, especially during the periods of adolescence and early adulthood. Only the naïve would infer from these facts that the Negro is made of inferior biological stock. All who work with him closely know that his illness and mortality rates are geared to health factors in his immediate environment. The Metropolitan Life Insurance Company reports on its policyholder experience for the period 1911 to 1935 by saying:

It is not difficult to see some reasons why mortality is higher among colored than among white persons. Generally speaking, the colored population is at a disadvantage economically, and as usual, this also brings with it the disadvantage of greater exposure to industrial risks, quite aside from the lower level of living.

So, despite the proverb, death, too, is a respecter of persons. Its heavy hand does not fall with equal frequency on youth of all colors and origins. It takes the poor youth before the rich one, the foreign-born before the native-born, and the colored youth before the white, for the art of life can be practiced well only when external circumstances are moderately favorable.

16

THE DAYS OF THEIR YOUTH

Expected Life Span of Negro and White Youth, at Age 20

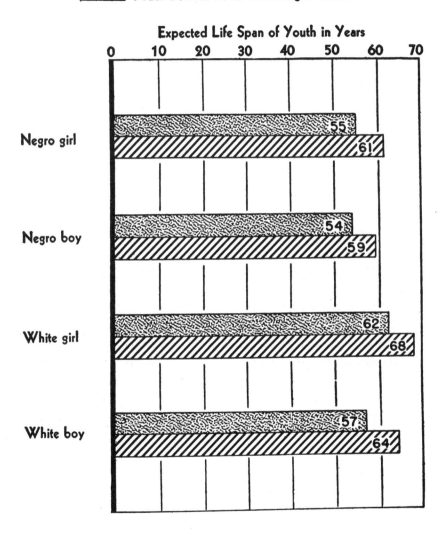

Youth born in 1891 and living in 1911

Youth born in 1915 and living in 1935

Expected Life Span of Youth in Years

1. Health is one of the more serious problems of the Negro population. The sickness and death rates from tuberculosis, pellagra, the hookworm disease, typhoid, diabetes, organic heart disease, nephritis, pneumonia, influenza, syphilis, and malarial fevers are high compared with those for whites.

2. The South is the only section of the country in which Negro births have consistently exceeded Negro deaths in the period 1933–36. Negroes in the West did not show an excess of births over deaths at any time during that period. States in which the Negro's death rate has been higher than his birth rate for each of these years are Maine, New Hampshire, Ohio, Indiana, Illinois, Minnesota, Iowa, Missouri, Nebraska, Kansas, Kentucky, Oklahoma, and all of the states in the Mountain and Pacific regions.

3. Since the date of the first census in 1790, and largely because of white immigration, the Negro population has increased about one-half as rapidly as the white. As a result, the proportion of Negroes in the population has decreased from one-fifth of the total in 1790 to approximately one-tenth in 1930.

4. The fertility of Negro women living in southern cities of more than 25,000 Negro population is from 30 to 40 per cent below that necessary to maintain the population permanently without immigration. The increase in net fertility among Negroes in most northern states may be attributed in part to improvement in health conditions and facilities, especially the lowering of infant mortality rates, and in part to the introduction into northern cities of many Negro families with the background and traditions of the rural South.

5. The Metropolitan Life Insurance Company reports:

There are $3\frac{1}{2}$ times as many deaths per 100,000 among colored females 15 to 19 years of age as among white females, nearly three times as many between ages 20 to 24, and $2\frac{1}{2}$ times as many between ages 25 to 34. Colored males show death rates $2\frac{1}{4}$ to $2\frac{1}{2}$ times as high as white males in these same age groups.

6. The National Health Survey of white and Negro populations in Atlanta, Dallas, Newark, and Cincinnati in 1935–36 revealed that in the 12-month survey period studied:

a. . . . the amount of disability per person due to illnesses which incapacitated for a week or longer was 43 per cent higher in the Negro than in the white population.

b. The higher disability rate for Negroes is due chiefly to the chronic diseases which disabled the average Negro eight days per year, compared with five days for the average white person.

c. Among Negro children under 15 years of age, the frequency of disabling illness was lower than among white children. . . .

d. Among adults . . . pneumonia was found to be almost twice as frequent among Negroes as among whites; and Negro rates for certain chronic diseases—the cardiovascular-renal group, rheumatism, asthma and hay-fever, nonmalignant tumors—were notably higher than those for the white population.

e. . . . the health problems of Negroes are more serious than those of the average white population since they represent in the mass a low-income group, unleavened, as in the white population, by any considerable number in the higher-income range.

7. The Committee on the Cost of Medical Care pointed out:

a. In 1925 it was estimated that the ratio of white dentists to the population was about one to 1,700; of Negro dentists to the Negro population, one to 8,500.

b. Negroes in the South suffer from a scarcity of hospitals.

c. The ratio of white physicians to population, in 1925, was one to about 800; of Negro physicians one to about 3,200.

Census statistics show that by 1930 there was one Negro physician for every 3,125 Negro inhabitants, one Negro trained nurse for every 2,076 Negro inhabitants, one Negro dentist for every 6,707 Negro inhabitants.

8. Negro women have a higher maternal mortality than white women, whether calculations are based on total women or total births at each age period. The excess colored over white mortality for each 1,000 live births runs from 70 to 100 per cent.

9. In the Metropolitan Life Insurance Company statistics for the period 1911–35, the excess mortality of colored policyholders over white policyholders amounted to 40 per cent among the males and 70 per cent among the females. Death rates are two or more times as high among colored policyholders as among white in the following diseases: influenza, tuberculosis, syphilis, cerebral hemorrhage, pneumonia, chronic nephritis, and homicide.

10. The death rate from influenza and pneumonia for the years 1931–35 was twice as high among colored persons as among white. Between the ages of 15 and 34 for each sex the rate for colored is three times that for white.

11. For organic diseases of the heart the death rate among colored persons exceeds that for white persons by 39 per cent among males and 64 per cent among females. Several reasons are given for these differences between the races, among them the relatively poor certification of causes of death, lack of medical attention, the incidence of syphilitic heart diseases, arduous work, and exposure.

12. Tuberculosis is a major cause of death in the Negro population and is still a scourge, especially in the younger age groups. For the 25-year period, 1911–35, the tuberculosis death rate for colored exceeded that for white by 86 per cent among males and 169 per cent among females. The death rate during this same period for colored persons in each sex exceeds that for white persons in every age period, but between the ages of 10 and 14 the colored death rate was more than ten times that of the white. For respiratory tuberculosis during the period 1931–35 the mortality of colored persons of both sexes under 20 years of age was about ten times as high as that among white persons.

13. Today the incidence of syphilis among Negroes is very high. The disease is imperfectly reported, yet the data indicate that the death rate among Negroes is about five times that among the whites. Between 1931 and 1935 the rate was four and a half times as high among colored men as among white and over six times as high among colored women as among white.

TUBERCULOSIS AND YOUTH

Death Rates per 100,000 of Each of Eight Sex-Race Groups

15 to 19 Years of Age

1911-15

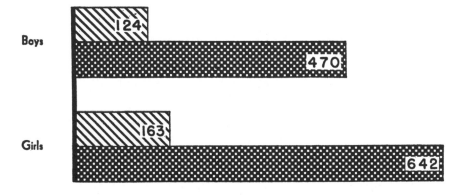

1931-35

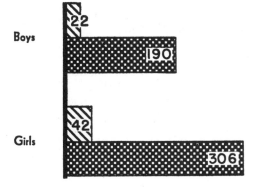

14. Too few data on infantile paralysis among Negroes are available to permit any sweeping generalization about racial differences and death rates. On this point the Metropolitan Life Insurance Company states:

The death rate for white persons exceeds that for the colored in this insurance experience. However, no great importance can be attached to this difference in the mortality among the white and the colored, since the total number of deaths among the latter in the experience covered by this study is relatively small.

15. Deaths from excessive heat are more numerous among colored than among white people.

16. For diphtheria and cancer the Negro death rates are below the white rates. Death rates for cancer and other malignant tumors in 1935 were lower for Negro males than for white males but higher for Negro females than for white females; but all rates are increasing.

17. Mortality from suicides is much lower among Negroes than among the white race. In the early-age periods, however, the colored rate is sometimes higher than the white, but after 25 years of age the relationship is reversed.

18. Mortality from railroad accidents among Negro males between the ages of 15 and 19 was almost three times that for the corresponding white group during the period 1931–35.

19. A colored male youth 20 years of age in 1935 had the prospect of living to the age of 59; a white boy of the same age might expect to live until he became 64 years of age. The average colored girl of the same age would live until she became 61, while the white girl has a seven-year longer life expectancy. If we should compare this with the outlook of youth 20 years of age in 1911, we should see that the average colored boy could then be expected to live to be 54 years old and the white boy to be 57; the colored girl might expect to live until she was 55, and the white girl until she was 62 years old.

III. NO PLACE LIKE HOME

Of parcels and estates, cabins and castles

NO PLACE LIKE HOME

N EGRO YOUTH emerge from a home environment filled with problems both social and cultural. Their families, in the main, do not have that long, unbroken set of rules and sanctions to keep them intact which characterizes some of the older white populations. Centuries of American slavery have left a deep imprint. Negro homes, all in all, are dreary dwellings, on neglected streets without pavements, littered by accumulated wastes, in the oldest residential sections of the city. The bulk of Negro youth live under just such conditions, but the range of the standards of the Negro family and the Negro home is as wide as that of any other group of similar economic and social levels in the American population. Being Americans, Negroes conform to the prevailing patterns of American living except where they are restrained from doing so by various social, legal, and economic handicaps, or by a lack of social training and low family standards, which, however, reflect earlier limitations in their experience.

You have seen the Negro district in your town. Why must Negro youth live in that section where the buildings are oldest, in extreme disrepair, hard to keep habitable, and impossible to sell except for industrial purposes? Do you know that in all probability the area in which Negroes live is potentially valuable for business purposes? That taxes are high? That rental costs and selling prices are generally quite exorbitant in relation to the incomes of people living there? While such basic factors are dominant, it is impossible to build new homes for occupancy by groups with such low incomes.

Harlem, originally a Dutch settlement, has been occupied by the Germans, the Irish, the Jews, and now by the Negroes. When

25

Negroes moved in rents went up. Because of the combination of economic factors mentioned above, added to the fact that colored people have less freedom in selecting their place of residence, Negro families often have to pay more for what they get than did the white families who evacuated the "area of invasion." That is, in certain metropolitan areas like Harlem, Negro families often pay more rent than do white families in the same income range. Thus, there arise new phases of social problems both of property rights and personal privileges, and the Negro is caught in the down-drag of the eddy which results.

Of course, taking the country as a whole, the average monthly rental paid by Negro families is much less than that paid by white families. In most sections of the country Negroes occupy the poorer sections of a town where the general rent level is low. Furthermore, if they move to better areas where rents are higher, the cost for individual or for family may still be relatively low because of doubling up—several families or one family and several roomers occupying what were originally single-family quarters.

Generalization on the housing conditions of the mass of the Negro population is difficult since the types of segregated areas in which Negroes live are limited only by the ingenuity of town planners and the disorder of sporadic city growth. But a summary of the chief characteristics might include:

Discriminatory limitation (through the pressure of public opinion or of real estate covenants) of the residential areas open to Negroes;

Enforced association of all types and classes of Negro individuals;

The tendency to municipal neglect of sections abandoned to Negro residents;

The lack of strict enforcement of sanitary regulations;

The disturbing indifference of Negroes themselves to these unfavorable conditions—which is, of course, in large part due to the

26

fact that the conditions are not only tolerated but actively perpetuated by the public authorities, the landlords, and the community at large.

Consider also the mortality rate from conflagration as reported by the Metropolitan Life Insurance Company for 1931–35 (italics by present writer):

Colored male policyholders exhibited a mortality rate from conflagration almost twice that for white males; the rate for colored females was $2\frac{1}{2}$ times that for white females. Excess colored mortality is in evidence at virtually every age. *Unsafe housing is partially responsible for the unfavorable position of the colored population.*

The notorious "rent houses" of the South, the "old law" tenements of New York, the alley-houses of Washington and Baltimore, the "ex-mansions" of Chicago, all of these help to feed that voracious ogre which is social disorganization. Negro families of means and position find it extremely difficult to secure comfortable homes in desirable neighborhoods; frequently they can neither buy nor rent in a decent locality. The devices of zoning laws, and the agreements of real estate concerns and property owners, keep them out of the better residential districts. Since courts are not supposed to uphold ordinances discriminating on racial grounds, zoning restrictions are not used constitutionally to segregate races. Through legal subterfuges they do, however, frequently achieve this end. Landowner compacts which in effect prevent the sale of property to Negroes have been upheld by some courts. Sometimes, white property owners have made life so unpleasant that the colored families invading the white area have been discouraged. This type of pressure was especially employed at the time of the race riots following the World War.

The vicious circle continues when, as Reuter says:

If by subterfuge they buy property in a desirable neighborhood it presently results . . . in neighborhood deterioration . . . . When Negro families move in, the whites move out, property values fall, deterioration takes place, and more Negro families move in. The first Negro families are frequently followed by a sporting element, from which they seek to escape and the neighborhood presently becomes a Negro slum.

In many of the northern cities the educated and more economically prosperous Negroes live in settlements away from the congested business district, in residence areas that do not differ in character from those of white families of similar economic status.

Under the slum-clearance projects and low-cost housing programs of the federal government, about 40,000 Negro families will be better housed—a program which will affect about one in every 100 Negro families. Until this program was initiated five years ago, only two ventures in housing programs for Negroes had been undertaken since the World War. The success of the Paul Laurence Dunbar Apartments of New York and the Boulevard Garden Apartments of Chicago gave example of and impetus to the development of such programs. Today low-cost housing facilities are available in limited quantity for Negroes in Atlanta, New York, Washington, Montgomery (Alabama), Louisville, Nashville, Indianapolis, and thirteen other localities, including the Virgin Islands.

Life within the homes of Negro youth is also conditioned by cultural and social factors. It is true that problems such as untimely death, desertion, illegitimacy, and other abnormalities related to health, crime, and morals appear with startling frequency within the Negro family group. It is likewise true that the average Negro home, urban or rural, is without many of the fundamental necessities for a minimum standard of economic and cultural decency. The presence of poverty may be reflected in family disorganization—laxity in sex and intrafamily relationships, improper care of children, and in parents working away from home. The instability of their homes may also affect the low fertility rates among Negro women. In nearly all regions where there are enough Negro women to make fertility rates reliable, the rate is lower for them than for native-white women. Add to these conditions the prob-

YOUR FAMILY AND MINE

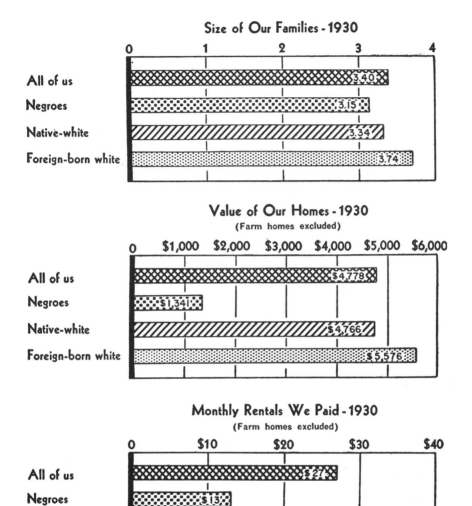

Size of Our Families - 1930

0	1	2	3	4

All of us — 3.40
Negroes — 3.15
Native-white — 3.34
Foreign-born white — 3.74

Value of Our Homes - 1930
(Farm homes excluded)

0	$1,000	$2,000	$3,000	$4,000	$5,000	$6,000

All of us — $4,778
Negroes — $1,341
Native-white — $4,766
Foreign-born white — $5,576

Monthly Rentals We Paid - 1930
(Farm homes excluded)

0	$10	$20	$30	$40

All of us — $27
Negroes — $13
Native-white — $28
Foreign-born white — $33

lems of race discrimination and there is little reason to wonder at the pessimistic outlook of many youth.

Despite all this, we may be sure that as the Negro is permitted increased participation in the life of the community great changes can be expected in the organization of his home life. Much of the chaos that now attends the Negro family's functioning is due to the changing conditions under which the Negro family must carry on. The future of our Negro youth can be filled with greater promise only as there is alteration of its present physical and social setting. Meanwhile, there is, perhaps, no place like home, but for all too many of our Negro youth that home is something rather worse than humble.

THE FACT

1. Believe it or not, in 1930 the median size of the Negro family (3.1) was smaller than that of the native-white family (3.3).

2. The value of real property owned by Negroes was estimated at $2,500,000,000 in 1935. That represents an approximate wealth of $210 per Negro.

3. It is harder to establish and maintain a Negro family than a white one, if we are to believe our 1930 statistics for every thousand persons 15 years of age and over in each of the following race and sex groups:

	Single	Married	Widowed	Divorced or Separated
Negro men	323	600	63	14
White men	341	603	45	11
Negro women	233	586	159	22
White women	268	614	105	13

4. Yet Negro youth marry earlier than do white youth. Of every 1,000 Negro boys between 15 and 19 years old in 1930, 37

were married; of every 1,000 white boys 15 were married. Within the same age groups 205 of every 1,000 Negro girls and 115 of every 1,000 white girls were married.

5. In 1930 every sixth Negro home, every tenth foreign-born white home, and every eleventh native-white home kept lodgers.

6. In 1930 more than 40 per cent of Negro families had two or more gainful workers. The chances of a married Negro woman's working outside the home are three and a half times greater than the married white woman's. Sometimes work is a blessing, but not when necessitated by low individual income.

7. From the point of view of home conveniences, the Negro family faces a gross economic inequality. There were radios in the homes of 403 in every 1,000 families of the total population, but in only 75 of every 1,000 Negro families. According to a sample study made in the South, only 22 in every 1,000 Negro families had radios in 1930.

8. About one-fourth (24 per cent) of all Negro families owned or were purchasing their homes in 1930.

9. Between 1933 and 1938 the Public Works Administration on 48 projects provided housing facilities for 7,478 Negro families, who formed 35 per cent of all rehoused families. Between 1939 and 1941 the U. S. Housing Authority will have provided in its low rental projects facilities for about 33,600 Negro families, who will form about 33 per cent of the total families to be housed in these new projects.

IV. LITERACY AND LEARNING

Of learning late deceased in beggary

LITERACY AND LEARNING

THE STORY

IN 1930 there were approximately 2,800,000 illiterate white persons in the United States, or about one in every 40. At the same time, about one in every six Negroes over 10 years of age, or approximately 1,500,000, were illiterate. Of this number, 250,000 were Negro youth between the ages of 15 and 24. Here we have one of the most challenging phases of the Negro youth problem. Looking backward to the days following emancipation from slavery, one sees that about 95 per cent of the adult Negro population were illiterate when they gained their freedom. Present-day figures, then, are indicative of remarkable improvement.

The major problem in the education of Negro youth today is one that is closely allied with the separate school system program of our southern states—the problem of adequate financing. A recent analysis of this subject shows that in eleven southern states the Negro youth receives 37 per cent of the amount to which he is entitled on the basis of an equal distribution of public funds, and his teachers on the average receive somewhat less than 47 per cent of the salary received by white teachers.

This problem, however, is not alone one of race. The section of the country in which most Negro youth are educated is less able to bear the cost of education than some other sections. In 1937 the average income in the South was $314; in the rest of the country it was $604, or nearly twice as much. In 1936 the state and the local governments of the South collected taxes on available wealth amounting to $28.88 per person, while the states and local governments of the nation as a whole collected $51.54 per person. During the same year the southern states spent an average of $25.11 per child in schools, or about half the average for the country as a whole. Thus the South has not had the funds with which to bring its schools up to national standards. While granting this fact, one cannot overlook the inordinate discrepancies that resulted in an annual expenditure (1930) in the South of $44.31 for white children and $12.57 for Negro children. In 1930 Negro youth received about one-fourth of the amount expended on white youth in the South and one-eighth of the amount expended on the average for youth in the country as a whole.

"By comparison with schools for white children," says Horace Mann Bond, "less money is spent for the public education of Negroes today than was spent in 1880." In 1880 when Negroes formed 40 per cent of the population of the southern states, Negro public schools received 25 per cent of all money spent for higher educational institutions, and 35 per cent of all money spent for elementary education. In 1930, when they comprised 25 per cent of the southern population, their schools received only 30 per cent of the higher education expenditures for its state-supported colleges and 10 per cent of all elementary school expenditures.

The consequent inadequacies in the education of Negro youth have induced philanthropists to help the states, and to encourage the continuing development of private institutions. Various funds, foundations, and church boards contribute millions of dollars annually for the support of rural elementary schools and private institutions at the secondary and college levels. And this form of subsidy is still necessary, because of the inadequate secondary and higher education facilities provided for Negroes by state funds.

Industrial education received its first major impetus among Negroes more than a century ago. The development of such schools as Tuskegee Institute and Hampton Institute represent the highest achievement in technical and agricultural education for Negroes.

36

EDUCATION FREE BUT NOT EQUAL

Expenditures for Public Elementary and Secondary Schools in Ten Southern States, 1935-36

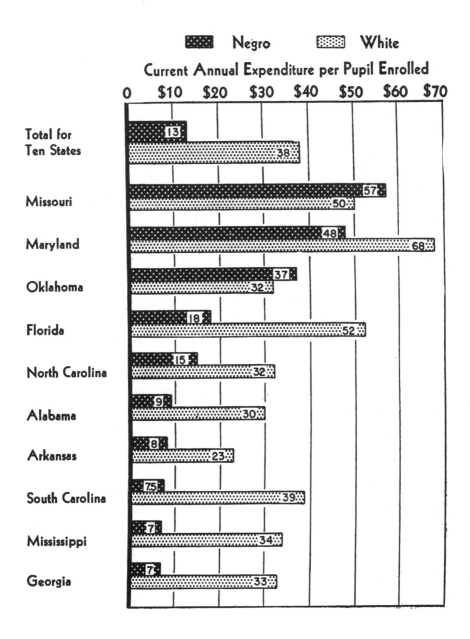

Negro   White

Current Annual Expenditure per Pupil Enrolled

0   $10 $20 $30 $40 $50 $60 $70

State	Negro	White
Total for Ten States	13	38
Missouri	57	50
Maryland	48	68
Oklahoma	37	32
Florida	18	52
North Carolina	15	32
Alabama	9	30
Arkansas	8	23
South Carolina	75	39
Mississippi	7	34
Georgia	7	33

Later the land-grant colleges were started with this type of education in mind, but changes have been made in many of these institutions. The major industrial schools have taken on liberal arts programs; and the 17 Negro land-grant colleges have enrolled many students of college grade (10,700 in 1937–38). Industrial education has lagged. Charles S. Johnson reports:

In the present period, when most city school systems boast at least one public technical high school of the finest type, the work in Negro schools is as a rule scarcely more than crude instruction in obsolete crafts and skills which are useless in a period of machine production.

Public education for Negro youth in the North also presents some difficult problems. Since 1917 throughout the United States there has been an increase in the number of communities where Negro youth are grouped in separate schools. Sometimes this has been done because the serious retardation of southern children constituted sufficient warrant for separate treatment, school authorities say. At other times it grows out of the high residential concentration of Negro youth. In still other situations the increasing demand for the employment of Negro teachers, who frequently are assigned to schools predominantly Negro in enrollment, has led to an increasing separation of Negro and white pupils, which many Negroes view with some apprehension.

The new life-conditions of Negro youth are demanding new methods and new types of adjustment from education. The public schools, the colleges, and the libraries are all called upon to meet this demand. Today these agencies are working toward creating new opportunities for Negro youth both in and out of school. Toward what goals should their efforts be directed?

THE FACT

1. Illiteracy of the Negroes in the South is high relative to that of the white people in the South, relative to Negroes in the North, and relative to the total population. In South Carolina and Alabama

in 1930 about one Negro out of every four was reported as unable to read or write.

2. Among the Negroes, as among the whites, the proportion of illiterates is smaller in the urban than in the rural districts. In 1920 the percentage of illiteracy among Negroes was 13.4 in the urban and 28.5 in the rural population; in 1930 the corresponding percentages were 9.2 and 22.4.

3. Between 1933 and 1937 projects of the WPA taught reading and writing to 400,000 Negro men and women past compulsory school age, thereby reducing adult illiteracy, it is estimated, by 30 per cent. In 36 states 4,000 Negro WPA teachers were engaged in this program.

4. The federal census of 1890 showed that among Negroes 10 years of age and over, 571 in every 1,000 were illiterate; the WPA estimate for 1936 indicated that 114 in every 1,000 were illiterate.

5. The National Youth Administration reports for the year ending June 30, 1939 that through its program 63,000 Negro youth between 16 and 24 years of age are receiving general education, practical training, guidance, work experience, healthful recreation, and more than $500,000 a month as direct work-aid benefits.

6. The Advisory Committee on Education appointed by the President of the United States in 1936 reported on the problems of Negro education as follows:

In most of the states where there are separate schools for Negroes, the schools for white children are below the national average, yet Negro schools are only about half as well supported as white schools. Because of the intimate economic relations that necessarily exist between the two races, the low level of education among Negroes is a severe burden not only on themselves but on all who must employ them or have dealings with them. Even in northern states, the large influx of Negroes from the South makes the quality of their previous training a matter of vital importance to the localities where they live and work.

39

7. In the North the school year is seldom less than 170 days. But in the South the school year for white children is often below the minimum in the North. The average school year for Negro children in 1936 (146 days) was 84 per cent of the average for the entire country (173 days) and 87 per cent of the average for white children in the South (167 days).

8. About 90 per cent of all Negro schools are of one-, two-, and three-teacher type, 64 per cent being one-teacher schools.

9. In each of the 18 southern states for which separate educational facilities are available, the percentage of children between 5 and 17 years of age in school is higher among whites than among Negroes. In 1936 the figures for the United States were about 85 per cent of the white and 83 per cent of the Negro children.

10. Though there has been a rapid increase in the number of public high schools for Negroes in the South (the number increasing from 91 in 1915 to almost 2,350 in 1936), less than one in every five is a standard and accredited institution. In 200 counties of the South having substantial Negro populations, there are still no four-year high schools for Negroes.

11. The United States Office of Education estimates that at least 900,000 Negroes of high-school age are not in school. In five southern states—Alabama, Arkansas, Georgia, Mississippi, and South Carolina—less than 10 per cent of the Negro population between 15 and 19 years of age was enrolled in high schools during the 1933–34 session. This ratio was much higher in Missouri, West Virginia, and Kentucky, where more than one-third of this age group was in high school, and highest in the District of Columbia, where half of the Negro youth were in high school.

Further information on school attendance is available in Chapter III of *Special Problems of Negro Education*, by Doxey A. Wilkerson.

12. In an effort to redirect the futures of Negro youth who were finishing work in northern high schools, and who were being forced

into many blind-alley occupations, the Vocational Survey Commission made the following recommendations for the New York City Public Schools:

Negro boys and girls should be admitted to vocational schools on the same basis as white children.

All school persons should have authentic information regarding Negroes in occupations.

Every effort should be made by counselors to induce employers to take a more liberal attitude toward Negro workers.

All counselors should be assigned for specific periods to visit industry and business.

Counselors in Negro districts should be selected for their special knowledge of the Negro situation.

The material in this survey should be kept up-to-date and should be amplified by staff members released for the purpose.

Every effort should be made to enforce strictly the attendance laws as they affect Negro children, especially between 15 and 17 years of age.

A sufficient number of junior high schools should be organized in Negro districts to accommodate all children of junior high school age.

A central guidance bureau for adults should be established in the Harlem district.

The Board of Education should continue to work out the problems of Negro education in cooperation with the bi-racial advisory committee which has cooperated in this survey.

13. NYA aid to students in 113 Negro colleges amounted to $520,420 during the 1937–38 scholastic year. In November 1938, 36,000 Negro students were being so aided.

14. Of the 42,300 students enrolled in 121 colleges and universities for Negroes in 1935–36 those registered for college courses number 35,000. The remainder were taking high school or elementary work.

15. The total number of living Negroes in 1932 who had graduated from college was approximately 19,000.

V. LIVING OFF THE SOIL

The Negro farmer's in a mess

LIVING OFF THE SOIL

THE STORY

No ASPECT of Negro life has been more completely disrupted within the last twenty years than that associated with agriculture. The Negro farm population of the South has declined and the average size of all Negro farms has decreased. The farm, once the bulwark of the racial economy, no longer welcomes youth.

Numerous factors have contributed to this decline in opportunity. Cotton, the mainstay of agriculture in the southeastern states where the bulk of Negroes live, has ceased being the reliable source of cash income it was some twenty years ago. Cotton's ill fortune has meant greater economic insecurity for the Negro—his reduction to hopeless peasantry in generally impoverished surroundings. In 1930 there were about 700,000 Negro tenant families in the South alone. These represent nearly 3,000,000 individual Negroes who have been affected by this change. So low is the estate of the cotton farmer that when the Farm Laborers and Cotton Field Workers' Union No. 20471 held a farm "wage" conference in Alabama in 1936, the full union wage scale was set for a ten-hour day as follows: chopping cotton, $1.50 a day; picking cotton, $1.25 a hundred pounds; picking peas, $1.25 a hundred pounds; general farm labor, $1.25 a day; wages by the month with meals, $20; wages by the month without meals, $26. None of these "high" standards has been met.

Within the past ten years farm workers' organizations have grown up throughout the South. They have set as their goal (1) the obtaining of the rights of share-croppers and tenant farmers to gin and sell their own cotton; (2) the right to trade where they please;

(3) the right to check and inspect their own accounts; (4) the right to receive government relief without the landlord's authorization; (5) abolition of the southern wage differential; (6) abolition of the poll tax; (7) federal support of education, free textbooks, better buildings, adequate transportation facilities; (8) the right to organize, meet, picket, strike, and bargain collectively; (9) cancellation of unjust debts and protection of croppers' and tenants' property against seizure for debt; (10) abolition of discrimination against colored workers in any of these proposals. These goals reflect the farmer's plight.

Even when the federal government poured vast sums into the South the results were not always beneficial to the Negro farmer. The new efforts to aid the farmer, based upon soil conservation, frequently seemed to offer less opportunity to help the tenant than the earlier Agricultural Adjustment Act. The Negro tenants are caught in the vicious circle of low income, low standards, and weak incentives to improvement. The wholesale losses in land values experienced by Negro farm owners between 1910 and 1935 bear eloquent testimony of the unrelenting rigors of an agricultural system which impinges upon white and black owners and tenants alike, making share-croppers of them all. Farm youth, meanwhile, trek to the cities.

THE FACT

1. In 1930, of every 1,000 Negroes gainfully employed who were 10 years of age and over, 361 were in some form of agriculture.

2. The big difference between the North and South is found in the division between the farm and nonfarm occupations. Farms hold 55 per cent of all gainfully occupied Negro males in the Southeast and 51 per cent in the Southwest, but only 7 per cent in the Northeast.

3. In 1930 less than 5 per cent of all gainfully occupied white women worked on farms, but 27 per cent of the gainfully occupied

Negro women and 22 per cent of those of other races were agricultural workers.

4. Only about one-fifth of the Negro farmers are owners or part owners of the land they cultivate; approximately four-fifths are tenants. In 1930, of every 1,000 Negro farmers some 158 were owners, 47 were part owners, 111 were cash tenants, 447 were share-croppers, and 235 operated under other forms of tenancy.

5. The percentage of Negro farmers owning their farms in 1930 was higher in the North and West than in the South. Ninety-nine per cent of the Negroes engaged in agricultural pursuits are in the southern states.

6. In 1900, the number of Negro farm operators including owners, tenants, and managers was 746,715; in 1910, the number was 893,370; in 1920, the number was 925,708; in 1930, the number was 882,850; by 1935, the number had decreased to 855,555. The latter figure includes all other than white people, about 95 per cent of whom are Negro.

7. In 1910 the valuation of all colored-owned farm property (and buildings) was $1,036,733,510; in 1935 the valuation of all farm land and buildings owned by colored farmers was set at $928,449,525. About 95 per cent of these colored farmers were Negroes.

8. Between 1920 and 1930 Negro farmers lost owned land to the extent of 2,749,619 acres, an area more than twice the size of the state of Delaware.

9. The National Resources Committee reports:

Colored farm families in the South have, on the average, much lower incomes than white farm families, but it would be a mistake to suppose that rural poverty in the South is a race phenomenon. The lowest average values, either of farm property or of farm productivity, frequently appear in areas where there are few colored people. . . . Nevertheless, average land values are distinctly lower in the South for farms operated by colored persons than for farms operated by whites.

10. Schuler's study of 167 southern Negro farmers in 1936–37 indicated that:

a. The Negro farm home averages 4.4 persons and 3.2 rooms. A southern white farm home averages 4.2 persons and 4.6 rooms.

b. Of his contributions to organizations the Negro farmer annually gives, on the average, 91 cents to the church and 8 cents to fraternal organizations. Less than one-tenth of one cent is spent for his economic advancement through farm organizations.

c. Ninety-eight per cent of these 167 Negro families studied have only kerosene light in their homes, and 32 per cent of them have no toilet facilities of any sort.

11. The federal Bureau of Home Economics in its 1935 study of consumer purchases among white and Negro farmers found that in North and South Carolina 42 per cent of the Negro operators and 35 per cent of the Negro share-croppers owned automobiles. In the same states 71 per cent of the white operators and 45 per cent of the white share-croppers owned automobiles. In Georgia and Mississippi 25 per cent of the Negro operators and 15 per cent of the Negro share-croppers owned automobiles as against 62 per cent of the white operators and 19 per cent of the white share-croppers. The same study also showed that in the Carolinas 14 per cent of the Negro farm operators purchased cars during the year; almost 90 per cent of these bought used cars at an average price of $197. Of the white farm operators 27 per cent bought cars, of which about half were used cars at an average cost of $311. Approximately 15 per cent of the Negro share-croppers bought cars and practically all of them were used cars at an average price of $173. About 18 per cent of the white share-croppers bought cars, of which about 85 per cent were used cars at an average price of $212. In Georgia and Mississippi the average price paid for used automobiles by white operators was $240; by Negro operators, $181; by Negro share-croppers, $85; and by white share-croppers, $80.

VI. RACIAL COMPETITION FOR JOBS

Othello's occupation's gone

RACIAL COMPETITION FOR JOBS

THE STORY

WHEN A noted European social scientist visited the United States some few years ago he observed that our industrial system was marked by a division of labor that harked back to the Middle Ages. Jews in small businesses, Irish in politics and on the police forces, Mexicans in the beet-sugar fields, Negroes in the cotton fields, native whites in the cotton mills, Italians on the laboring and construction jobs, Poles in the tobacco fields and cranberry bogs, and Greeks in the restaurants showed the result of occupational segregation by race, nationality, and religion. As a matter of broad interpretation, André Siegfried was partially correct. Certainly he was accurate so far as the employment of Negroes was concerned, for in the development of industry and occupations in this country, Negroes, only recently removed from slavery, found certain occupations theirs by right, by sufferance, and by experience. "Negro jobs" were jobs done by Negroes, jobs that Negroes were expected to do, jobs that other workers—especially native-white workers—would not do. In 1890 these jobs were legion; in 1939 they were few.

The grandfathers of contemporary Negro youth were caterers and cooks, barbers and valets, coachmen and footmen, butlers and waiters, for personal service was one of the special provinces of the Negro. In the South some were brick masons, plasterers, carpenters, and painters—even contractors. Slavery had given them a heritage of special skills. Domestic service, being beneath the dignity of all white workers, was monopolized by Negroes in the South.

51

Then changes came. White immigration introduced many new workers; cotton mills were established in the South and employed white labor. Women bobbed their hair, and preferred white beauticians. The automobile replaced the carriage and introduced thousands of white-operated filling stations. Then depressions and machines cut the need for as many workers as we had; trade and labor unions developed, and excluded or outbargained Negro workers. Immigration stopped; migration started. Industry slowed down. Then shirts—the Ku Klux Klan, Black Shirts, Silver Shirts, even "stuffed shirts"—arose and paraded. "Blood is thicker than water!" "Give jobs to white men and women!" they cried.

Today the only jobs in which Negroes have a virtual monopoly—the only ones in which the Negro is still free from competition with white workers—are those of Pullman porter and dining-car waiter.

Negro youth look at this scene with mixed emotions and a sense of confusion. They know that if rationality and justice are eventually to prevail, the race factor in job allocation must be eliminated from our economic ideology. But this idea seems touched with irony for many a Negro who can find no job whatever. If there has been something of a blessing in the decline of the philosophy of segregation implicit in the old system of Negro job monopolies, existing conditions of unemployment and underemployment have given any such blessing an impenetrable disguise. To Negro youth, the gradual disappearance of "Negro jobs" has meant, temporarily, at least, being pushed out at the bottom of the occupational market.

General economic breakdown has filled the lives of white workers also with cataclysmic disturbances. The whole social environment to which the Negro youth must make adjustment is one of stress and strain, of conflict and psychosis. Maddening frustration, compensatory vindictiveness, ruthless striving, and impassioned idealism are finding organized expression all about him. There are organizations of the unemployed, the employed, the employers. There are socialist, communist, fascist organizations; Negro-rights

WHEN THE MANNA FAILETH

Employment Status by Age-Race Groups, 1937

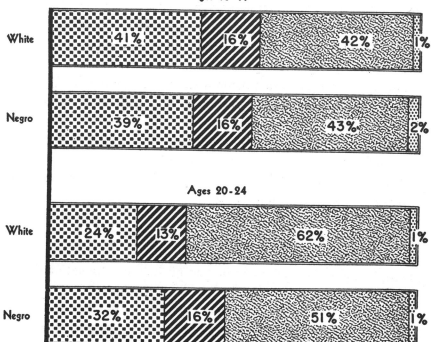

groups, white-supremacy groups. There are organizations of share-croppers and workers, owners and renters, of "fat cats and starved rats." From every quarter there are organized attacks on things as they are and sharply conflicting efforts to change them. Negro youth—many of whom, because of the depression, have never been able to find places for themselves in our social economy—must face the many ordeals of a society in travail under all the special handicaps which have gone to make up their group heritage. Unless they find doors of opportunity in what appears to many of them to be the blank wall of Tomorrow, their lot is one of hopelessness. In brief, Negro youth seeking economic security face the following handicaps:

They must live down a tradition of slavery.

Frequently they do not obtain promotion on the job.

When there is prosperity and plenty of work, there are opportunities for Negroes at the bottom of the employment scale. In times of unemployment, the pressure on this bottom drives Negroes out of industry.

The restrictive membership practices of trade and labor unions frequently prevent successful competition for jobs.

Inefficient preparation for skilled work, even when employment is available, is still a problem.

THE FACT

1. The Negro formed 11.3 per cent of the country's employed in 1930 although his population was only 9.7 per cent of the whole.

2. In 1930, 5,500,000 Negroes were gainfully employed.

3. The masses of Negro workers were distributed as follows in 1930: 2,000,000 in agriculture were 19 per cent of all the farmers; 1,600,000 in personal and domestic service, were 32 per cent of all those in these occupations; 1,000,000 in manufacturing, were 7 per cent of the workers in this field; 900,000 in all other occupations.

4. Increasing job competition has upset the traditional balance of employment between whites and Negroes in the South. Unemployment among whites has sent them scurrying to seek jobs traditionally filled only by Negroes. The *Report on Economic Conditions of the South* states: "The field for the employment of Negroes has consequently been further constricted, causing greater migration. The lack of opportunity and the resulting job competition has lowered the living standards of both white and Negro worker in the South."

5. Negro carpenters, bricklayers, and contractors have been displaced on a large scale by white workers in the South.

6. In comparison with white skilled workers, Negro artisans and building trade craftsmen provide only one-third of their proportion of the working population.

7. The occupational status of Negro women in the North has changed little in twenty years. In the South there has been a change from agriculture to domestic and personal service.

8. Let us glance at the way unemployment affects colored youth, 95 per cent of whom were Negroes (determined by the November 1937 Unemployment Census, based on enumeration of 32,692 colored youth):

a. Eighteen per cent of all colored youth 15 to 24, and 31 per cent of all colored youth in the labor market, were totally without work in November 1937.

b. An additional 2.2 per cent of all colored youth, or 3.8 per cent of colored youth in the labor market, were employed only on emergency work, making 20 per cent of all colored youth, or 34 per cent of all in the labor market, who were either wholly unemployed or employed only on emergency work.

c. Nine per cent of all colored youth, or 16 per cent of those in the labor market, were working part-time in regular employment.

Of these, about nine-tenths (86 per cent) wanted more work and may be considered partly unemployed.

d. Thus unemployment among colored youth, counting those who were wholly unemployed, partly unemployed, and employed only on emergency work, amounted to 29 per cent of all colored youth, or 50 per cent of all colored youth in the labor market. The corresponding figures for white youth between 15 and 24 years are 24 and 44 per cent.

e. Twenty-eight per cent of all colored youth, or 48 per cent of those in the labor market, were working full-time in regular employment.

f. Thus, 37 per cent of all colored youth, or 64 per cent of those on the labor market, were working either full- or part-time in regular employment; and counting in emergency employment there were 40 per cent of all colored youth and 68 per cent of those on the labor market who had some kind of employment.

g. Almost 2 per cent of colored youth on the labor market were ill or voluntarily idle.

9. The Maryland youth survey in 1936 found the median weekly wages of 1,029 employed Negro youth to be $7.98, and of 4,474 employed white youth to be $14.33. Eighty-one per cent of the Negro youth worked more than 30 hours during the week preceding the interview and averaged $8.88; the corresponding figures for white youth were 87 per cent and $15.48.

Sixty per cent of the full-time employed Negro youth received less than $10 a week; 22 per cent of similarly employed white youth were in this wage range.

The Maryland male Negro youth averaged 49 hours a week and received $8.71. The corresponding figures for 2,826 white male youth were 44 hours a week and $15.17. The female Negroes (329) worked 44 hours and received $6.35 while the female whites (1,648) worked 41 hours and received $13.20. These are median values and include all out-of-school employed youth.

10. The WPA study of youth in the labor market of seven large cities found in Birmingham, Alabama, that a sample of selected Negro youth averaged $7.91 a week, whereas white youth similarly selected received $16.14 a week.

Thirty-one per cent of the Negro youth in the labor market were currently unemployed, whereas 22 per cent of the white youth were unemployed.

Only 11 per cent of the Negro youth had been continuously employed at private jobs of 15 hours or more a week, while 31 per cent of the white youth had been so employed.

11. The Maryland youth survey revealed that for farm youth the employed Negro male averaged almost as much as the white male: the former averaged $8.06 a week, the latter, $8.94 in cash wages.

The wage differences were not large except for the older age group, 22 to 24. Negro farm youth 16 to 18 years of age averaged $5.69 a week; white farm youth of the same ages, 19 cents more a week. Negro farm youth 19 to 21 received $8.26 a week while white farm youth of the same ages received $3.20 more than the Negro youth.

The wage situation was strikingly different for the farm female youth, the white girls averaging at every age slightly more than twice that of the Negro girls. For ages 16 to 24 the former received $10.80 a week, the latter, $4.71.

The difference between the sexes as well as that between the races is largely an occupational one. Male youth, whether white or Negro, were in large measure working on farms, fisheries, etc., where wages are low and apparently not greatly different for the two races. White girls who live on farms, if gainfully employed, are working in town or city as clerks, stenographers, or teachers, and hence tend to receive a higher wage. Negro female farm youth were engaged for the most part in domestic service and received the low pay associated with those occupations.

VII. THE NEGRO PROFESSIONAL

White collars and "best people"

THE NEGRO
PROFESSIONAL

THE STORY

SOCIAL LIFE in the Negro group is a struggle for higher status—individual and racial. It is a highly artificial and limited situation, of course, but one that is imposed upon the group by the dominant white majority. Nearly all Negro education is directed toward the "white-collar" occupations—and, largely because these occupations are the jobs of leadership and of greatest remuneration within the Negro group, they are the jobs in which Negroes will face a minimum amount of competition from white workers; they are the jobs that more nearly insure the recognition of individual ability.

The 1930 federal census figures show that approximately 46 in every 1,000 Negro workers were in the "white-collar" class, that is, were employed in professional, proprietary (excluding farmers), official, managerial, or clerical pursuits, and in such other occupations as are characterized chiefly by the exercise not of brawn but of mental ability. In 1910 only 27 of every 1,000 Negro workers were so engaged. But compare this change with that of the total population in which the number of white-collar workers per 1,000 total workers was 207 in 1910 and 298 in 1930.

The depression made serious inroads into Negro business, particularly the retail business. The payroll of these establishments dropped from $8,528,000 in 1929 to $5,021,000 in 1935. During the same period the total sales of these stores dropped from $101,146,000 to $48,987,000 or by more than half.

Incomes from Negro business are small. A national study of consumer purchases showed that the median yearly incomes of Chicago families for 1935–36 in which the principal earner was engaged in an independent business was $1,459 for the native white, $1,408 for the foreign-born white, and $721 for the Negro. These estimates included relief and nonrelief families. For families not on relief the figures were $1,518, $1,454, and $799 respectively. Thus, "being in business" does not necessarily mean that Negro proprietors make enough money to follow standards of middle- or upper-class living.

Salaried and fee workers and entrepreneurs have suffered diminished incomes during recent years. The financial misfortunes of those whom they serve are reflected upon this class of workers.

If Negro youth show a desire to go "white collar," there is no need to fear that the professions will be overcrowded. In most fields the problem of too many Negro professionals does not exist; the problem is, rather, one of unbalanced distribution. A large part of the Negro population is still rural and southern; most of the professional classes are urban and northern. Whether, how, and where the twain will meet is the problem.

When compared with the distribution of occupations among the white population, the only Negro group in which there appears to be no need for further increase is the ministry. This is the only vocation of professional character in which the number has been considerably higher for Negroes than for white persons. Of growing importance in the professional field is the employment of Negroes in government positions, in jobs as librarians, as social workers, as entertainers and actors on the stage and screen, and as musicians—sweet, swing, and serious.

Women are becoming increasingly important in the professional life of the Negro population. Forming approximately 45 per cent of the Negro white-collar population, they contribute to this group

THE WORK PATTERN

By Occupation and Race - 1930

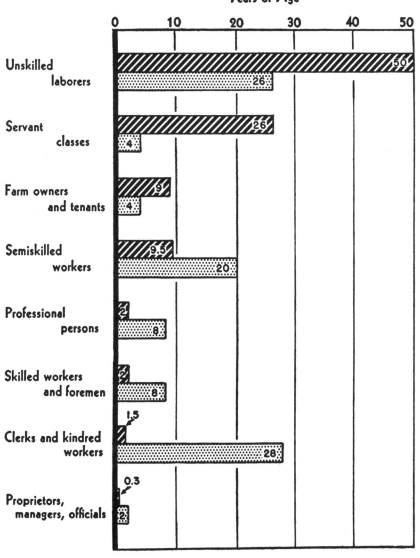

four-fifths of all the school teachers, librarians, and social workers, and more than half of all the actors, artists, and entertainers.

White-collar workers do not represent the masses of the Negro population; they are the "best people." They have been trained at Harvard and Yale, at Atlanta and Howard. They send their children to college and professional schools. They belong to monthly book clubs, attend the theaters, go to Europe, and follow fads and fashions even as do the "best people" in white society.

THE FACT

1. Negro enterprises providing services to the Negro population, such as barber shops, shoe repair shops, undertaking establishments, beauty parlors, and cleaning, dyeing, and pressing shops, numbered 22,172 in 1935. They did a business totalling receipts of $27,281,000 during that year. The average receipts for an establishment was $1,230 in the United States; $1,449 in the North; $1,097 in the South; and $1,010 in the West.

2. Retail stores operated by Negroes in 1935 numbered 23,490. These enterprises gave employment to 36,141 persons, and had a total payroll of $5,021,000.

3. In 1936 twenty-three Negro banks and savings institutions were reported with a total capitalization of $2,000,000 and resources of approximately $15,000,000.

4. The economic problem attending Negro professional classes is not so much one of excessive number as of unequal distribution. Statistics indicate that employment for professional work for Negro women is lowest in the Northeast and in the Middle States regions, and greatest in the South.

5. Negro professional classes increased 50 per cent between 1920 and 1930, but the ratio of professionals to the population is

still considerably less than in the white population. In the white population of native parentage 7.2 per cent of gainfully employed persons are doing some form of professional service; in the Negro population the professional group covers only 2.1 per cent of the gainfully employed.

6. The ministry is the only profession in which there are relatively more Negroes employed than whites. Among Negroes in 1930 there was one clergyman for every 475 of their population. Among the white population there was one clergyman for every 885 persons.

VIII. RELIEF AND RECOVERY

They toil not, neither do they spin

RELIEF AND
RECOVERY

THE STORY

T HE MARGINAL nature of the Negro's economic status made him the barometer of the employment decline during the ten depression years, 1930 to 1939. In February 1939 it was estimated that approximately 400,000 Negroes were receiving government aid through WPA alone. In 1936, when Negroes already made up one-sixth of the depression relief rolls, they were being added to those rolls in a proportion twice as great as were white persons. Yet, they were removed from the relief rolls through re-employment only half as frequently as were white persons.

Behind this economic upheaval lay multiple causes. A few may be summarized as:

The dislocation of the tenant system in agriculture;

The displacement of Negro workers by white labor;

The widespread wage differential discriminating against Negro workers;

The lack of provision for Negro unemployables.

The extent of the relief problem among Negro families is indicated by the fact that in 1933, in the states of more than 100,000 Negroes, 18 per cent of the Negro population was on relief as compared to 10 per cent of the white population. Of the states having more than 100,000 Negroes in their population only Mississippi, Arkansas, West Virginia, and Kentucky had a higher relief percentage for white than for Negroes. Even in these latter cases it is not to be concluded that the need was greater among whites than among Negroes. A number of special circumstances, plus certain inequalities in relief procedure, affect the published figures. Relief discriminations have been more marked against rural than urban Negroes. The Works Division of WPA has reported difficulty in administering work relief for Negroes in an area where farm laborers receive 75 cents a day for fourteen hours' work and rural relief clients receive $2.40 for an eight-hour day. Farm relief for Negroes has been seriously abused and reflects the influence of social tradition in keeping the status of the Negro rural worker on a lower plane. Manifold instances demonstrate that the credit system and the "furnishing system" endured by share-croppers perpetuate shamefully low standards of living. They direct attention to basic problems of that whole economic situation in which Negroes have experienced a thus far unbroken bondage.

American youth on relief in 1935 constituted 14 per cent of the number of youth recorded in the 1930 census. Fifteen per cent of the urban youth and 13 per cent of the rural youth were on relief; 14 per cent of white as compared with 17 per cent of Negro youth were on relief. In the District of Columbia, where Negro youth formed 30 per cent of the total youth population in 1930, they formed 80 per cent of the youth relief population in 1935. States showing an exceptionally high ratio of Negro youth on relief were: Texas, South Carolina, Ohio, New Jersey, Missouri, Massachusetts, Indiana, and Delaware.

The National Youth Administration has done much to offset racial discrimination in the relief administration of many southern states, especially in cities. The federal government has made efforts to see that relief is administered without discrimination and to see that Negroes are included in the "reform" programs. In spite of these efforts, the Social Security Board's study of age, sex, and color in a 10 per cent sample of the applicants for account numbers, as of December 1937, revealed that only 274,813 of the 3,613,022 applicants were Negroes. Male Negroes formed 6.2 per cent of all applicants and female Negroes 1.4 per cent of the total; hence Negroes were 7.6 per cent of all applicants, though they were 11.3 per cent of all the 1930 gainfully employed. Thus, a relatively much smaller number of Negroes have applied for the protection of the Social Security Act. This is not due, however, to discrimination in administering the act, but rather to the fact that the act itself does not cover those occupations where the bulk of all Negro workers are employed: namely, farm labor and domestic service. A Social Security Board sample indicated that 14 per cent of the new applicants for the first half of 1938 were Negroes.

The outcome of the present relief and recovery program is difficult to predict. It is true that many Negroes are now receiving more from the relief program than they ever received in private employment. To urge them back to such low-paid jobs as those to which they have been accustomed would hardly be consistent with the general policy of our federal government. The plight of the Negro on relief may be regarded as a barometer of recovery and a guide to certain much-needed social and economic reforms.

THE FACT

1. Approximately one-sixth of the population of the United States was on relief—wholly or partly—in May 1935. In 1938, it was estimated that between 3,500,000 and 4,000,000 of the 11,000,000 Negroes in the population were receiving some form of government relief.

2. Negro youth, though they number but 105 per 1,000 of the total youth population, numbered 153 per 1,000 of the youth population on relief. If relief were administered more consistently on the basis of need in the southern states, it is reasonable to conclude that the relief ratio of Negro youth would be much higher.

3. Approximately 200,000 colored youth have served in the CCC from April, 1933 to July, 1939. For the year ending June 30, 1939,

these youth have supplemented their family incomes by about $600,000 a month.

4. Of 54,480 transients, age 16 to 24, receiving help in May 1935, 4,900 were Negro. Only 31 per cent of Negro transient youth had gone beyond the eighth grade, as compared with 52 per cent of white youth.

5. Of the 36,000 Negro students receiving NYA aid in 1938, 25 per cent were from families where the parent or guardian was either totally unemployed or working on WPA. The average annual family income of these Negro students was $623 as compared with $1,163 for all students aided by NYA.

6. The Social Security Board reports:

Negroes form a considerably smaller proportion of the 10 per cent sample than they did of the gainful workers in 1930. This difference is not surprising since many Negro workers are employed in excepted occupations. The recent applications, however, have tended to increase the proportion of Negroes among holders of account numbers.

7. In November 1938 approximately 63,000 Negro youth were employed on the Student Aid and Works Program by the NYA. This number represented 11 per cent of the 591,000 youth aided by NYA.

IX. LEISURE AND PLAY

Leisure for recreation and idleness for loafing

LEISURE AND PLAY

KENNY WASHINGTON, Joe Louis, John Henry Lewis, and Henry Armstrong are just a few of the young Negroes who have recently won distinction in the world of sports. Jesse Owens, Ralph Metcalf, Dehart Hubbard, Paul Robeson, Duke Slater, Ned Gourdin, Fritz Pollard, and Matt Bullock were among the Negro youth of yesteryear who also played well in their respective fields. Negro athletes have won acclaim in many fields, but their individual successes have only served to high-light the problem of play, recreation, and leisure for Negro youth. The problem is not alone one of recreational facilities such as playgrounds, parks, recreational centers, social settlements, theaters, and commercial amusement parks, but it is also a problem of public attitudes and established conventions.

Recreation facilities for Negro youth throughout the country are woefully inadequate. In some communities the problem of recreation for Negroes is utterly ignored, while in others it receives only passing attention. Such attention as has been given to the need has been in most cases only recent, and has not appreciably altered the pattern of inequality. One cannot expect the average Negro home, impoverished and inadequate as it has been shown to be, to provide the appropriate setting for the development of ability to make good use of leisure time. In areas of racial segregation the public schools do not meet the need for effective training in the use of leisure time, and they are, of course, sadly deficient in play equipment. Generally speaking, Negro youth's specialized recreational facilities are limited to:

75

Cities where Negro youth are relatively unrestricted in their social movement—as in the East and Midwest;

Cities that have provided some type of playground and public recreational facilities especially for Negroes;

Cities having Negro high schools that have encouraged the development of play activities;

Cities in which Negro colleges have encouraged athletic programs.

Utilization of leisure has been so neglected among Negroes that their play life has largely been confined to two forms: (1) uncontrolled and unorganized random activity on the part of cliques, and passive time-wasting on the part of individuals, and (2) commercial recreational activities as a cheap substitute for the lack of socialized facilities in the Negro community.

Expression of the first type of activity is at once a survival of the Negro's rural heritage and a compensation for the lack of organized leisure activities in urban areas. The fishing, hunting, "doing nothing," "lying around," and "just talking" of the rural youth become the fishing and hunting and "night-clubbing" of the less impecunious urbanite. The same "doing nothing," "hanging around," and "loafing" form the recreational pattern of the moneyless urbanite who finds the street corner, the "barbecue joint," the "chicken shack," the barber shop, and the pool room places of least discomfiture and greatest relaxation. What else is there to do? There must be some outlet for the disturbed emotions attending city life. The unique niches formerly filled by the church and the school in a less highly organized community have no adequate counterparts in areas of new concentration. In most cases, unsupervised commercial recreation has taken over these functions.

Youth of no other racial community in the United States are so completely dependent upon some form of commercialized recreation for fulfillment of their leisure-time needs as are Negro youth. This most impoverished group of youth finds its major recreational outlet in fields demanding the use of dollars and cents. The swimming pool, the subscription dance, the pool room, the "joint" with an electric talking machine playing the latest recording of popular song and dance music, the beer parlor, the night club, the "gyp joint," the cabaret, the movies: all of these point to the lack of organized recreation in the Negro community. Chicago's South Side and New York's Harlem provide striking examples of this phenomenon. So great has grown this type of activity that, along with restaurants, grocery stores, barber shops, and beauty parlors, commercial recreation is one of the most important parts in the economic structure of the Negro community.

The Young Men's Christian Association, the Young Women's Christian Association, and the Boy Scouts of America have been the recreational saviors of our modern Negro youth. A few cities with active recreation commissions, a few settlement houses and community house programs, and the general planning of activities of the Playground Association of America have prevented the utter demoralization of the leisure-time aspects of Negro life. And, ironic as it may seem, the depression (through the leisure-time organizations made possible by the extraordinary dispensations of public funds, particularly through WPA and NYA) has given Negro youth more constructive leisure-time programs than they have ever had before.

THE FACT

1. In 12 southern states (Alabama, Arkansas, Florida, Georgia, Kentucky, Louisiana, Mississippi, North Carolina, South Carolina, Tennessee, Texas, and Virginia) having in 1930 a Negro population of 8,633,437, some 7,138,455 Negroes, or 83 per cent, had in 1935, no access to a public library.

2. In 1935 there were 509 public libraries in 13 of the southern states (those mentioned in "1," above, and West Virginia). Yet

77

only 94 of this number served Negroes. In Mississippi, where there are more than one million Negroes who form more than half of the state's population, only two of the state's 22 public libraries were open to them in 1935.

3. "Of 12 state library plans examined in 1935 only four incorporated recommendations for extending equality of library service to Negroes."

4. The Bureau of Labor Statistics study of money disbursements among 897 white and 100 Negro families in New York City during the period 1934–36 showed that the white families with an average net annual family income of $1,745 and averaging 3.65 persons spent approximately $113.63 annually for recreation. The Negro families with an average net family income of $1,446 and averaging 3.13 persons spent $82.29 annually for recreational purposes. The items covered by these amounts included reading materials, tobacco, commercial entertainment, recreational equipment, recreational associations, and entertaining in the home (except for food and drinks).

5. The following facts summarize the leisure-time facilities available during 1935 (in areas where separate facilities are provided):

Colored branches of the Young Men's Christian Association and the Young Women's Christian Association provided either gymnasiums, swimming pools, game rooms, and vocational classes or other leisure-time activities in more than 60 cities. Settlements and community centers for Negroes existed in approximately 40 cities.

Boy Scout troops were found in more than 200 cities and towns of the North and South.

In 66 cities and towns the Girl Scouts or Camp Fire Girls had special troops for Negro girls.

6. On the optimistic side is the fact that 139 communities are providing special or exclusive facilities for the recreation of colored youth in the United States.

7. According to the National Recreation Association, there were in 1930 "hundreds of other cities . . . where cooperative or bi-racial uses of recreation centers made playgrounds available."

8. Communities providing recreational facilities for colored people increased nearly 200 per cent between 1925 and 1935. A check-up on recreational buildings in 1935 revealed "eighteen additional centers particularly set apart for the use of colored groups, and an increase of 49 play areas."

X . LET US PRAY

The church sees its ancient verities questioned, its paradise lost; it looks "right" and eases "left"

LET US PRAY

NEGRO YOUTH emerge from a racial environment that has been religious and Protestant for nearly two centuries. The churches of their race have long served as more than places of worship—they have been centers of the social and cultural life of the Negro community. Their pastors have long been more than ministers—they have been teachers and leaders in all "safe" programs for the improvement of the racial lot. The churches were the first places of free assemblage for Negroes. Here were championed the issues of slavery and of justice for the Scottsboro boys. Their ministers first led the movements in the South for a truckling racial peace, then followed their migrating congregations to more northern climes. In religion—the church, the denomination, and the minister—the Negro found a kind of peace and an outlet for the expression of all his social interests and aspirations.

Today the role of the Negro church has changed. The rural background and traditions of Protestantism have been crumbling. The mobility of Negroes and their increasing urbanism, changing conditions of housing, work, relief, and rapid social change generally, have presented great problems of adaptation to the Negro's church. Once almost entirely Baptist or Methodist, the Negro community is now showing unmistakable signs of a stronger leaning toward the Catholic church, toward certain newer denominations, and toward various "cults." For the first time old-fashioned Protestantism is lagging. Once the church had a family constituency. Now the boy may go to the Y. M. C. A., the girl to the Y. W. C. A., and the parents listen to the popular radio preacher or the "Southern-aires" and "Wings Over Jordan."

The church is said to have lost in numbers and in general influence. A more economics-conscious young Negro population charges that the church tends to be capitalistic in its sympathies and religious only in its exhortations. That type of church has been declining in its importance. No longer able to maintain its missionary-society program of charity and prayer, it has been unable to keep pace.

On the other hand, there are indications that a new church is arising among Negroes—a militant church, one that is concerning itself with the problems of the masses. Sometimes it is the old-line Protestant church, sometimes a younger denomination, sometimes a Catholic congregation—and sometimes a community church. Its leaders organize and take part in aggressive social movements for the public and the race's weal. Led, in a few urban and rural centers, by outstanding men who are trained and practiced in religion as well as economics, this church is vital. Yet it cannot be said that even today this church is an influential factor in the lives of the whole Negro working population.

Extremely significant in Negro life, however, has been the inordinate rise of religious cults and sects. Even before the depression, one noted this tendency in Harlem where there were:

Bishops without a diocese; those who heal with divine inspiration; praying circles that charge for their services; American Negroes turned Jews over-night; theological seminaries in the rear of "railroad" apartments; black Rev. Wm. Sundays, Ph.D., who have escaped the wrath of many communities; new denominations built upon the doctrine of race—all these and even more contribute to the prostitution and disruption of the church. . . .

Today, Father Divine, Elder Michaux, Daddy Grace, Moslem sects, congregations of Black Jews and the Coptic Church have been added to the church organizations existing among Negroes. Their influence and reach are enormous and significant—perhaps more

LET US PRAY

Reported Membership in Negro Churches, 1926

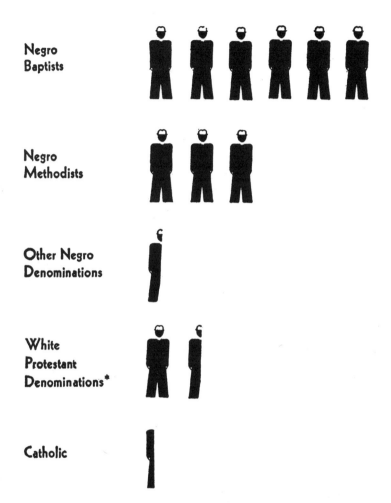

Negro
Baptists

Negro
Methodists

Other Negro
Denominations

White
Protestant
Denominations*

Catholic

Each symbol represents 500,000 reported membership

*Members in Negro churches affiliated with Protestant denominations predominantly white

socially adapted to the sensationalism and other unique character-istics of city life, and the arduousness and bitter realities of race, than the prayerful procrastinations of the church institutions they now supplant.

In the past, the Negro's church has had tremendous influence along two lines. It has initiated and patterned Negro higher educa-tion to a remarkable degree, and it has served as the organized group through which many programs for race relations have been initiated. But, as Negroes advance in education and as larger numbers move into the larger culture, the Negro's church as it has been functioning, "picturing a future existence free from the real and imaginary shortcomings of the present order," will pass. The new Negro's church is just coming of age. It and today's Negro youth will face the problems of survival and progress together.

THE FACT

1. The Negro's church has been the greatest racial organization in his social life; yet its individual leadership has been the least trained of all the professions. Fry's analysis of the 1926 federal census of religious bodies showed that nearly three out of every eight ministers in the eighteen leading white denominations and more than three out of four of those in the three leading Negro bodies were not graduates of either a college or a seminary.

2. There is a church for every 178 adults among Negroes and one for every 340 among whites. Five out of every 12 Negroes in the United States claim membership in some church.

3. In 1926, the membership reported by the Negro Baptists was over 3,000,000; the four Negro Methodist bodies report a member-ship of slightly over 1,500,000; the Roman Catholic Church reports about 124,000 members, and the Protestant Episcopal Church a little over 50,000. In membership, the sexes maintain a ratio of

approximately 60 men to 100 women. Approximately 75 per cent of the Negro churches and about 60 per cent of the membership are rural.

4. At the time of the Emancipation there were perhaps 700,000 Negro church members most of whom held their membership in white churches. One-half of the number were Baptists and four-fifths of the remainder were Methodists.

5. In the aforementioned 1926 federal census of religious bodies approximately 43,000 Negro churches and 5,000,000 Negro church members were reported. This membership was 9.5 per cent of the total church membership in the United States.

6. There are 24 entirely Negro church denominations and 30 denominations having both white and Negro churches.

7. The average annual contribution per Negro church member in 1926 was $9.15. White church members averaged $19.54 annually.

8. Church membership varies by race and sex. For the population 13 years of age and over 73 per cent of Negro women, 62 per cent of white women, 49 per cent of white men, and 46 per cent of Negro men are counted on church rolls.

9. The Negro's church is the race's largest property owner. In 1906 when 23,770 churches were enumerated the value of Negro church property was approximately $27,000,000. By 1926, when churches increased to 37,347, the value had increased to $206,000,000.

XI. THE EVIL MEN DO

Of crimes and arrests, prosecutions
and convictions, mobs and lynchings

THE EVIL MEN DO

THE STORY

N O ONE need try to deny that for the country as a whole and for most communities the rate of convictions for Negroes is considerably higher than for whites. Although Ernest Hooton may still be looking for a racial explanation of this condition, most sociologists have tried to explain the fact in the type of conditioning influences surrounding the development of Negro youth. When large numbers of people moved from country to city during the industrialization process which swept this country, many individuals—white and colored— failed to adjust to the new environment. The Negro suffered particularly because he had so little contact with urbanization in the past, and because he moved in such large numbers when the call for labor was made by northern cities at the close of the World War. Socially he was poorly prepared to cushion the shock of his new urban experiences. That is to say, the illiteracy and inadequate educational background which many of the migrants brought with them increased the problems of adjustment to an impersonal and individualistic urban environment.

Social maladjustment in general and the crime problem in particular are not, however, limited to the urban setting, nor to the migrant individual, but are a common accompaniment of life in nearly all Negro communities. As long as there exists in the United States a public opinion which perpetuates an unequal opportunity for the social development of minority groups, and so long as there exist economic insecurity and substandard conditions of living for large numbers of people, high crime rates are to be expected. Debarred from many occupations, forced to live under a class and caste-like system supported by common sanction if not by law, and in districts that are conducive to crime, Negro youth fall easily into antisocial patterns of conduct. Clifford Shaw's studies have indicated that regardless of their race or nationality any group, living in areas where criminal patterns have become traditional, shows abnormally high rates of crime until it is able to move to more organized neighborhoods. Racial prejudice enters as another complicating factor, since arresting officers as well as court officials are frequently less considerate of the Negro criminal than of the white. Also, since many Negro youth have inadequate funds for defense attorneys, the rates of conviction are relatively high.

In summarizing the crime problem of the Negro one student points out that Negro youth receive less education and training; that, because of their poverty, their housing and living conditions are more deplorable; that there is less provision made to care for colored defectives; that they are in a more or less unstable condition because they but lately gained their freedom, and many of them—especially in the cities and in the North—are in a new and strange environment; that they are discriminated against socially and industrially; that they are often abused by the police; and that, sometimes, at least, they are not fairly treated in the courts.

THE FACT

1. The proportion of arrests, commitments, and convictions is much higher for Negroes than for whites. On January 1, 1933, the proportion of prisoners present in county and city jails was 128.5 to 100,000 Negro population and 38 to 100,000 native-white population.

2. Of the 53,768 native-born whites and Negroes committed to federal institutions between July 1, 1931 and June 30, 1937, 7,989, or 15 per cent, were Negroes. The commitment rate (for 100,000

THE EVIL MEN DO

The Ratio of Total, Negro, and Native-White Prisoners
per 100,000 of 1930 Population 15 Years of Age and
Over in County and City Jails, January 1, 1933

All persons

Native-whites

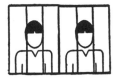

Negroes

Each symbol represents 20 persons per 100,000 population of that race

population) of Negroes to federal institutions in 1936 was about two times that of whites.

3. The two offenses for which Negroes are most frequently committed, and to which they contribute as high as two-fifths of all the offenders, are homicide and assault.

4. The death rate among colored boys between 15 and 19 years of age from the use of firearms is nearly twice as high as that among the white boys of the same ages. During the period 1931 to 1935 it was 9 for colored and 5 for the white. During the period 1911 to 1935 the rate was 14 for colored and 6 for white.

5. Homicide is an alarming cause of Negro mortality. During the 25-year period, 1911 to 1935, about seven times as many colored as white persons were slain, based on 100,000 population. Between the ages of 25 and 34 there were 104 deaths for each 100,000 colored males as against 12 deaths for each 100,000 white males. The greatest disparity occurs in adolescence, when over ten times as many colored as white youth are slain. The following states had a homicide death rate of more than 50 per 100,000 colored population between 1929 and 1931: Ohio, Illinois, Michigan, Missouri, Nebraska, West Virginia, Kentucky, Tennessee, Wyoming, Colorado, and Florida.

6. From the most accurate sources of information, it is found that in the 55 years, 1882–1936 inclusive, there were 1,190 persons (97 white and 1,093 Negroes) put to death by mobs under the charge of rape or attempted rape. This is 25 per cent of the total number of persons, 4,672, who were lynched during that period. On the other hand, 3,482 or 74 per cent—that is, three-fourths of those lynched—were for causes other than rape. This refutes the charge that the majority of lynchings are for the crime of rape.

7. An investigation into the causes of lynchings shows that over 10 per cent of the Negroes lynched in the period 1882 to 1936 were for such minor offenses as being a witness, writing insulting notes,

94

improper conduct, insisting on eating in a restaurant when refused service, threatening man with a knife, trying to act like a white man and not "knowing one's place," being a strikebreaker, using insulting language, striking white man in quarrel, discussing a lynching, making boastful remarks, misleading mob, vagrance, slapping boy, jumping labor contract, insisting on voting, gambling, incendiarism, throwing stones, and enticing servant away.

8. One of the most encouraging aspects of the vanishing American lynch scene is change in the ratio of the persons lynched to the number of lynchings prevented in the United States. In 1914 there were 52 persons lynched and 24 persons prevented from being lynched. In 1936 eight persons were lynched and 79 lynchings were prevented.

XII. THE LAW

We must not make a scarecrow of
the law

THE LAW

THE STORY

THIS IS A MELANCHOLY TALE. While the Negro strives to improve the conditions under which he lives, he increasingly finds his progress hampered by the letter, sometimes by the spirit, often by the interpretation of the law—be it federal, state, or municipal. Many laws in the United States are specifically designed either to abrogate and restrict, or to establish and protect the rights of Negroes. Examination reveals the limitation of franchise, the unequal distribution of public funds for education, the denial of social, civil, and personal rights supposedly guaranteed by the federal Constitution and laws—all these are notorious and menacing commentaries on what it means to be a Negro in the United States.

The Thirteenth, the Fourteenth, and the Fifteenth Amendments to the Constitution guarantee certain basic rights and privileges. The Thirteenth Amendment abolished slavery. The Fifteenth Amendment states that rights of citizens to vote shall not be denied or abridged because of race, color, or previous condition of servitude. The Fourteenth Amendment is of special interest since it provides for "due process of law" and "the equal protection of the laws":

No state shall make or enforce any law which shall abridge the privileges or immunities of citizens of the United States, nor shall any state deprive any person of life, liberty, or property without due process of law, nor deny to any person within its jurisdiction the equal protection of the laws.

To prevent deviations from these fundamental tenets 19 states have passed civil rights laws to reaffirm those rights specifically

99

set forth in the Constitution. For twenty years efforts have been made to pass a federal antilynching bill but thus far without success.

What, then, are the legal limitations upon the Negro individual? When he becomes 21 he may not vote in the primaries of ten states. The "white primary," the poll tax, educational tests, the "grandfather clause," and the demand that two white persons vouch for every Negro who wishes to register as a voter, are among the chief means of taking the vote from the Negro.

In 15 states from the day of his birth the Negro is segregated with unequal accommodations in public conveyances and in public places. In these states, trains and buses, streetcars and taxis, all provide separate facilities for Negroes and in most instances decidedly inferior ones to those offered for the same prices to white passengers. If a Negro asks for Pullman accommodations in many southern states the chances are great that he will be refused altogether or given "Lower 13" (the lower berth in a compartment or drawing room) with the expressed or implied instruction that he must keep the door to the compartment closed, and not enter the dining car for his meals. In some of these states it is impossible to secure sleeping-car accommodations.

If the Negro wants an education he must attend separate schools in 18 states and the District of Columbia. Certain northern cities also provide separate facilities for Negroes. In almost no instance are the outlays for staff or equipment of the separate schools for Negroes equal to those for whites.

If the Negro wants to live in a better residential area, with cheaper rents and better protection than are available in the usually old and congested Negro section, he may find restrictive covenants barring his way.

Because the United States Supreme Court has ruled that a Negro has not been convicted by due process of law, before a jury of his peers, when he has been convicted in a court where Negroes are barred from the jury, a few Negroes have been included on jury

THE DECLINE OF LYNCHING

Lynchings of Negroes in the United States, 1890-1938

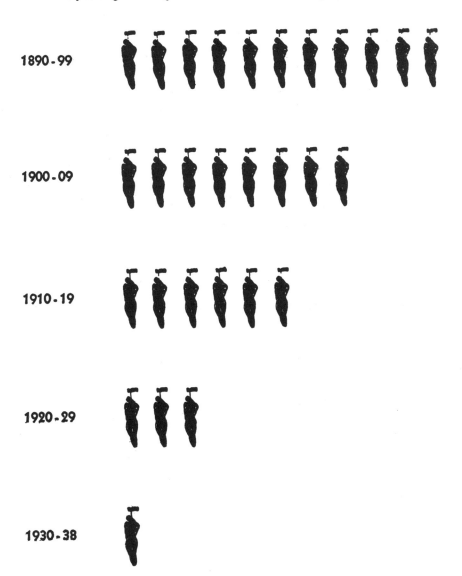

1890-99

1900-09

1910-19

1920-29

1930-38

Each symbol represents approximately 100 lynchings

panels in southern states during the last few years—especially since the famed Scottsboro case. But, in general, this decision continues to be disregarded.

Finally, an adult southern Negro is taxed without representation. In northern states, he may not be disenfranchised, but his neighborhood is often discriminated against in the inadequate facilities of water, sanitation, police, and property protection that are provided. Of all the violations of civil rights in the United States those affecting Negroes are by far the most numerous and diverse.

THE FACT

1. Segregation in schools and public conveyances, a denial of the right to vote, and a ban on interracial marriage are found in the following states:

Alabama	Mississippi
Arkansas	North Carolina
Florida	Oklahoma
Georgia	South Carolina
Louisiana	Texas

2. All of the restrictions above except disenfranchisement are invoked in:

Kentucky	Tennessee
Maryland	Virginia

3. All of the states above, together with Delaware, Missouri, and West Virginia enforce school segregation and ban interracial marriage. Separate schools are required also in the District of Columbia.

4. The following states also have interracial marriage bans:

California	Nevada
Colorado	North Dakota
Idaho	Oregon
Indiana	South Dakota
Montana	Utah
Nebraska	Wyoming

XIII. PLANNING FOR SURVIVORS

For work does good when reason fails

PLANNING FOR
SURVIVORS

THE STORY

THE "RACE PROBLEM" cuts a wide swath in the cultural heritage of Negro youth as their people have moved away from the complete subordination of slavery into a state of theoretical freedom. Problems of adjustment and conflicts of interests between white and Negro races have arisen with perplexing consistency. Each new situation and each new condition has demanded some new adjustment and some new compromise, for there are no ready-made final solutions for maintaining inequalities or for keeping a race "in its place." Charles S. Johnson ventured the opinion that:

It is, perhaps, because our form of government, in principle, at least, is democratic, that so many conflicts arise between what every citizen has the right to expect, and what is deemed expedient for the Negro citizen to have. Their former status as slaves, together with a habit of thinking about them as permanent inferiors, no doubt have considerable influence upon present-day race relations.

Yet, before Negroes have an opportunity to know or understand the why of the problem, they learn that circumstances have necessitated movements for controlling, regulating, and improving these relations between the races. While these movements are in most instances less than 30 years old, they represent the common ground where all people may work mutually for the amelioration and obliteration of the social ills affecting this generation. This search for justice, and the finding of it, bear witness to the fact of progress in human relations.

There are a few fairly well-defined programs designed for reaching this end. One program is directed toward advancing the economic, educational, and occupational status of the Negro group. Another program is directed toward removing the blight of race through the use of propaganda, publicity, and legal action; toward securing full legal and social rights for Negroes immediately. More recently younger Negroes have combined with younger whites in seeking Utopian democracy through political action based upon socialistic and communistic principles. Again, there are the religious and quasi-religious groups that have sought to reach the goal through programs of good will. Also, there are the distinct intraracial movements built to increase a racial solidarity against the intolerant attitudes and discriminatory practices of white people, and to create a pride of accomplishment, a confidence, and a spirit of independence among Negro groups.

Above all, there must be considered the will and activity of the total Negro group itself. Whenever a minority learns to use its political power to achieve desirable ends in a democracy, it has taken one major step toward becoming socially virile and progressive. Illinois has a Negro representative in the Congress of the United States. In states of the East and Midwest the political power of the Negro is an important factor in municipal and state politics. Negro legislators have served in the parliamentary bodies of New York, New Jersey, Pennsylvania, Illinois, Indiana, Ohio, Kentucky, and West Virginia. In 1939 Pennsylvania sent its first Negro woman to the state legislature. Elective and appointive positions in the public service are held by Negroes in every major city of the North. All of these movements must be regarded as significant for the future of Negro youth, for the role of the Negro in American life is not yet fixed; and regardless of what the final outcome will be, that outcome will be determined by the will of the public.

Increasingly it is being noted that the problem of Negro youth is not one of race alone, but a broadly human one. Too many Negro

PHILANTHROPY LENDS A HAND

Foundation Gifts to Negroes

1921 $ $ $

1922 $ $ $ (

1923 $ $ (

1924 $ $ $

1925 $ $ (

1926 $ $ $ (

1927 $ $ $ (

1928 $ $ $ $ $ (

1929 $ $ $ $ $ $ $ $ $

1930 $ $ $ $ $ $ $ $ $ (

Each symbol represents $500,000

youth and white youth are poor together, ignorant together. Negroes have been victimized because of their low plane of living and little economic independence. They have appeared servile because they have been oppressed; they have been oppressed because they were poor. As we advance in culture and estate, new philosophies, new insights, and new understandings of the economic and social complexities of our living will appear. New programs will be devised to meet and implement these new philosophies. The need of preparation for this advance is the challenge to Negro youth and to those interested in his welfare.

THE FACT

Welfare organizations intended to benefit all youth are too numerous to be adequately summarized in a one or two-page statement. Since Negro youth gain some benefit from many of these agencies and are further aided by organizations or branches of organizations intended for their special assistance, the most useful set of facts that can be given in this chapter is a list of the private and public institutions which are dealing in one way or another with the Negro youth problem and whose specific program of work can in most cases be secured from the agency's headquarters.

Federal Agencies
Washington, D. C.

DEFENSE HOUSING COORDINATION
> Robert R. Taylor, *Consultant to Division of Defense Housing Coordination**

FEDERAL SECURITY AGENCY
> CIVILIAN CONSERVATION CORPS
> > Edgar G. Brown, *Adviser on Negro Affairs*
> NATIONAL YOUTH ADMINISTRATION
> > Mary McLeod Bethune, *Adviser on Negro Affairs*

OFFICE OF EDUCATION
Ambrose N. Caliver, *Senior Specialist in Negro Education*

PUBLIC HEALTH SERVICE
Roscoe C. Brown, *Health Education Specialist and Director of the National Negro Health Week Program*

SOCIAL SECURITY BOARD, BUREAU OF EMPLOYMENT SECURITY
Lawrence A. Oxley, *Supervisor, Negro Placement Service*

OFFICE OF PRODUCTION MANAGEMENT
Robert C. Weaver, *Administrative Assistant, Division of Labor Supply**

FEDERAL WORKS AGENCY

PUBLIC WORKS ADMINISTRATION
William J. Trent, Jr., *Racial Relations Officer*

U. S. HOUSING AUTHORITY
Frank S. Horne, *Acting Director of Racial Relations**

WORK PROJECTS ADMINISTRATION
Alfred Edgar Smith, *Adviser on Negro Problems*

WORK PROJECTS ADMINISTRATION, EDUCATION DIVISION
James A. Atkins, *Specialist in Negro Education*

SELECTIVE SERVICE SYSTEM
Campbell C. Johnson, *Executive Assistant**

UNITED STATES DEPARTMENT OF AGRICULTURE

AGRICULTURAL ADJUSTMENT ADMINISTRATION, SOUTHERN DIVISION, TUSKEGEE INSTITUTE, TUSKEGEE, ALABAMA
Albon L. Holsey, *Head Field Officer*

FARM CREDIT ADMINISTRATION
Cornelius King, *Special Assistant to the Governor*

FARM SECURITY ADMINISTRATION
Constance Daniel, *Information Specialist on Negro Problems*
Giles Hubert, *Agricultural Economist*

UNITED STATES DEPARTMENT OF COMMERCE

BUREAU OF THE CENSUS
Joseph C. Houchins, *Specialist in Negro Statistics*

UNITED STATES DEPARTMENT OF WAR
William H. Hastie, *Civilian Aide to the Secretary of War**

111

* Brought up to date, second printing.

Private Agencies Rendering Specific Aid to Negro Projects and Promoting Interracial Welfare

Agency	*Purpose*
AMERICAN SOCIAL HYGIENE ASSOCIATION 50 W. 50th Street New York City	To join with federal and other official agencies and with voluntary groups in the promotion of social hygiene activities. These include: informing the public about the venereal diseases, providing wholesome and constructive public entertainments for youth and adults as substitutes for vice, and providing sound sex education in its broad sense for childhood and youth.
AMERICAN YOUTH COMMISSION 744 Jackson Place Washington, D. C.	This is a commission of the American Council on Education. The Council is an alliance of national educational organizations and institutions. The Commission was established in 1935 to conduct a comprehensive investigation of the problems facing young people in the United States. It is concerned not only with the problems of in-school youth, but also with the care and education of millions of youth whom the schools are not now reaching. It is publishing a series of studies on these problems.
AMERICAN YOUTH CONGRESS 55 W. 42d Street New York City	Its program stands for the abolition of child labor, the passage of the American Youth Act, to provide work and educational opportunities for unemployed and out-of-school youth, the organization of unorganized working youth into trade unions, the passage of the Nye-Kvale Bill to abolish compulsory military training in schools and colleges, the expansion of the student strike against war, and the freedom of the press and freedom of teaching.

112

Agency	Purpose
BIG BROTHER AND BIG SISTER FEDERATION, INC. 425 Fourth Avenue New York City	To promote the welfare of children and the saving of boys and girls from delinquency by individual and personal effort through special volunteer organizations and through cooperation with other agencies, using methods which are now in common use by Big Brother and Big Sister organizations, and to act in an advisory capacity to such various volunteer organizations as are now in existence, and to cooperate wherever and whenever possible with such organizations or similar organizations.
BOYS AND GIRLS 4-H CLUBS United States Department of Agriculture, Extension Service Washington, D. C.	"The 4-H Clubs are organized to help rural girls and boys to do something worthwhile in homemaking and agriculture . . . to develop into wholesome, worthy manhood and womanhood in keeping with the ideals indicated in the 4-H Clubs' insignia."
BOY SCOUTS OF AMERICA Stanley Harris, *Secretary for Negro Work* 2 Park Avenue New York City	"The purpose of this corporation shall be to promote, through organization and co-operation with other agencies, the ability of boys to do things for themselves and others, to train them in Scoutcraft, and to teach them patriotism, courage, self-reliance, and kindred virtues, using the methods which are now in common use by Boy Scouts."
COMMISSION ON INTERRACIAL COOPERATION W. W. Alexander *Executive Director* 710 Standard Building Atlanta, Ga.	To correct interracial injustice, to better conditions affecting Negroes, and to improve those interracial attitudes out of which unfavorable conditions arise. The Phelps-Stokes Fund has sponsored the Commission.

Agency	*Purpose*
FEDERAL COUNCIL OF THE CHURCHES OF CHRIST IN AMERICA George E. Haynes, Katherine Gardner, *Race Relations Secretaries* 105 E. 22d Street New York City	To secure effective cooperation among the Protestant churches in local, state, and national areas; to develop a spirit of larger unity; and to serve as a center through which the churches can unitedly work with the social, interracial, and international problems of common concern.
FRIENDS SERVICE COMMITTEE 20 S. 12th Street Philadelphia, Pa.	The activities are carried on through (1) a Social-Industrial Section, which conducts rehabilitation projects in bituminous coal fields, operates a series of "work camps" for young people in volunteer service jobs in connection with settlement camps and other social institutions; and (2) Peace and Foreign Service Sections.
GENERAL EDUCATION BOARD 49 W. 49th Street New York City	To promote education in the United States without distinction of race, sex, or creed. The present program of the Board is restricted, in the main, to giving assistance to the following: research and experimentation for the improvement of general education, chiefly on the secondary and junior college levels; education in the Southern states including, especially, assistance to Negro education; and training of personnel for research and teaching in fields wherein work is undertaken jointly with the Rockefeller Foundation.
GIRL SCOUTS, INC. 570 Lexington Avenue New York City	"The purpose of this organization is to help girls to realize the ideals of womanhood, as a preparation for their own responsibilities in the home and (for) service to the community; in the realization of

this purpose the corporation shall be the directing and coordinating head of the Girl Scout Movement in the United States, its dependencies and possessions, and shall fix and maintain standards for the movement which will inspire the rising generation with the highest ideals of character, conduct and attainment."

JULIUS ROSENWALD FUND
4901 Ellis Avenue
Chicago, Ill.

To promote the well-being of mankind. The chief programs are promotion of rural education; Negro welfare; cooperation in pay clinics and medical service for people of moderate means; and to aid the study of educational and social problems, especially in the area of race and culture.

METHODIST EPISCOPAL
    CHURCH, BOARD OF HOME
    MISSIONS AND CHURCH
    EXTENSION
1701 Arch Street
Philadelphia, Pa.

The activities most closely related to social are identified with the Bureau of Goodwill Industries, employing more than 15,000 handicapped people; the Bureau of Negro Work; the Departments of City and Rural Work, including Indian Activities; and work in the mountain districts of Kentucky, North Carolina, and Tennessee.

NATIONAL COUNCIL OF
    STUDENT CHRISTIAN
    ASSOCIATIONS
347 Madison Avenue
New York City

"The Student Christian Movement is a fellowship of students who, seeking the meaning of life, are captivated by Jesus and His understanding of God and Man and are committed to comprehending and following its implications in personal and social living."

NATIONAL FEDERATION OF
    SETTLEMENTS
147 Avenue B
New York City

To reinforce all phases of federated activity among neighborhood agencies, to bring together the results of settlement experience throughout the country, to secure capable recruits, to urge measures of state and national legislation suggested by settlement experience, and to promote the better organization of neighborhood life generally.

NATIONAL RECREATION
   ASSOCIATION
Ernest T. Atwell, *Represen-
   tative for Colored Work*
315 Fourth Avenue
New York City

To promote a program whose purpose is that every child in America may have a chance to play, and that all persons, young and old, may have an opportunity to find the best and most satisfactory manner of using leisure time. To obtain or develop more children's playgrounds, neighborhood play fields, etc.

NATIONAL TUBERCULOSIS
   ASSOCIATION
50 West 50th Street,
New York City

To study tuberculosis in all its forms; to disseminate knowledge concerning causes, treatment, and prevention of tuberculosis; to stimulate, unify, and standardize the work of various anti-tuberculosis agencies throughout the country, especially the state and local associations; to cooperate with all other health organizations in the coordination of health activities; and to promote international relations in connection with health activities in the study and control of tuberculosis.

PHELPS-STOKES FUND
101 Park Avenue
New York City

The Fund has devoted its major attention to the improvement of Negro education and race relations in the United States and Africa, and the improvement of New York City housing conditions. A survey with special reference to New York City entitled *Slums and Housing* was published in 1936.

Agency	Purpose
YOUNG MEN'S CHRISTIAN ASSOCIATION Channing H. Tobias, *Senior Secretary for Colored Work* 347 Madison Avenue New York City	To minister to the needs of Negro boys and young men in and out of school, helping them meet the problems and conditions of present-day life and giving them opportunities for greater self-development of body, mind, and spirit. A positive program is offered for the teaching of character-making ideals, by the promotion of health education and physical activity, by providing opportunities for intellectual self-improvement, by acquainting boys and young men with the teaching and ideals of Jesus, and by providing wholesome, social fellowship and economic and vocational guidance.
YOUNG WOMEN'S CHRISTIAN ASSOCIATION Isabel Lawson, *Secretary for Colored Work* 600 Lexington Avenue New York City	"The immediate purpose of this organization shall to be to unite in one body the Young Women's Christian Associations of the United States; to establish, develop, and unify such Associations; to participate in the work of the World's Young Women's Christian Association; to advance the physical, social, intellectual, moral, and spiritual interests of young women. The ultimate purpose of all its efforts shall be to seek to bring young women to such a knowledge of Jesus Christ as Savior and Lord as shall mean for the individual young woman fullness of life and development of character; and shall make the organization as a whole an effective agency in the bringing in of the Kingdom of God among young women."

Agencies Specifically Interested in Problems of Negro Folk

Agency	*Purpose*
AMERICAN TEACHERS ASSOCIATION H. Councill Trenholm, *Executive Secretary* State Teachers College Montgomery, Ala.	To improve educational conditions among Negroes; to influence public opinion in support of the education of Negroes; to equalize salaries of teachers in white and Negro schools; to secure the enactment of teachers' tenure and retirement laws by the several state legislatures.
ASSOCIATES IN NEGRO FOLK EDUCATION Alain Locke, *Secretary and Editor* 1326 R Street, N. W., Washington, D. C.	To prepare materials on Negro history, life, and culture for the use of adult education groups. Nine syllabi to be prepared as follows: (1) World Aspects of the Race Problems; (2) The Economic Side of the Race Question; (3) The Negro and His Music; (4) The Art of the Negro; Past and Present; (5) The Negro in American Drama; (6) The Negro in American Fiction and Poetry; (7) Social Reconstruction and the Negro; (8) An Outline of Negro History and Achievement; (9) Experiments in Negro Adult Education.
ASSOCIATION OF COLLEGES AND SECONDARY SCHOOLS FOR NEGROES L. S. Cozart, *Secretary-Treasurer* Barber-Scotia College, Concord, N. C.	To develop the colleges and secondary schools for Negroes and to maintain helpful relations between them.
NATIONAL ASSOCIATION FOR THE ADVANCEMENT OF COLORED PEOPLE Walter White, *Secretary* 69 Fifth Avenue New York City	To combat the spirit of persecutions which confronts the colored people and other minority groups in the United States and to safeguard their civil, legal, economic, and political rights, and secure for them equality of opportunity with all other

citizens. Junior branches and youth councils are organized throughout the country.

NATIONAL ASSOCIATION OF
COLORED WOMEN
Mary F. Waring, *President*
1114 O Street N. W.
Washington, D. C.

To raise to the highest plane the home life, moral standards, and civic life of the race. The work is carried on through departments that reach the individual women and clubs, through sectional and state chairmen. Better homes, education, health and hygiene, social service, and women in industry are now being emphasized.

NATIONAL CONGRESS OF
COLORED PARENTS
AND TEACHERS
Leonidas S. James,
Executive Secretary
State Teachers College
Bowie, Md.

To promote child welfare in the home, school, church, and community; to raise the standards of home life; to secure more adequate laws for the care and protection of women and children; to bring into closer relation the home and the school that parents and teachers may cooperate intelligently in the training of the child; to develop between educators and the general public such united efforts as will secure for every child the highest advantages in physical, mental, moral, and spiritual education.

NATIONAL NEGRO CONGRESS
John P. Davis, *Secretary*
717 Florida Avenue, N. W.
Washington, D. C.

To coordinate and unify the efforts of the Negro organizations and friends of Negro freedom in their attempt to win full social and economic rights for the Negro. The congress supports and initiates campaigns to organize Negro workers, to improve the status of Negro women and youth; and aims to educate both Negro and white public opinion to workers' problems.

Agency	*Purpose*
NATIONAL URBAN LEAGUE Eugene Kinckle Jones, *Executive Secretary* 1133 Broadway New York City	To make investigations among Negroes in cities, to promote social work among Negroes until other agencies extend their programs to include them, to conduct activities through the League machinery until a demonstration is made and the whole work is assumed by some other agency; to provide for the training of Negro social workers. (Competitive scholarships are available.) To further the industrial advancement of the Negro. (Branches in cities.)
NEGRO RURAL SCHOOL FUND ANNA T. JEANES FOUNDATION 726 Jackson Place, N. W. Washington, D. C.	To promote the improvement of Negro rural schools. Counties are aided to employ supervising teachers to visit small rural schools in order to help and encourage the rural teachers; to introduce simple home industries; to promote the improvement of school houses and school grounds; and to organize clubs for the betterment of the school and neighborhood.

Negro Collegiate Fraternities and Sororities

Chapters of these youth organizations are to be found at the leading colleges and universities. Alumni chapters are usually found in the larger cities.

Fraternities

Alpha Phi Alpha   Phi Beta Sigma
Kappa Alpha Psi   Omega Psi Phi

Sororities

Alpha Kappa Alpha   Iota Phi Lambda
Delta Sigma Theta   Sigma Gamma Rho
Zeta Phi Beta

120

AUTHORITIES
FOR THE FACTS

AUTHORITIES FOR THE FACTS

PREFACE
"A new race . . ."
Edwin R. Embree, *Brown America* (New York: Viking Press, 1931), pp. 3, 24.

I. TO BEGIN WITH

Page 5. Their Numbers Are Increasing
Negroes in the United States 1920–1932 (Washington: U. S. Bureau of the Census, 1935), pp. 1, 92. Also *Population Statistics: 1. National Data* (Washington: National Resources Committee, 1937), p. 12.

Page 9. Going to Town
Negroes in the United States 1920–1932, p. 7. Also *Thirteenth Census of the United States, 1910. Population*, Vol. I (Washington: U. S. Bureau of the Census), p. 184.

Page 10. 1. The number of Negro youth per thousand youth is from Scripps Foundation estimates for 1940 based on medium fertility, medium mortality, and no net immigration. *Population Statistics: 1. National Data*, pp. 9–12. Maine and Mississippi data from *Negroes in the United States 1920–1932*, p. 108.

Number and percentage of Negroes in 1930. *Ibid.*, p. 1.

In these statistics, "South" is used as in the federal census. It includes Alabama, Arkansas, Delaware, District of Columbia, Florida, Georgia, Kentucky, Louisiana, Maryland, Mississippi, North Carolina, Oklahoma, South Carolina, Tennessee, Texas, Virginia, and West Virginia.

2. *Ibid.*, p. 1.

3. *Ibid.*, p. 92. See also *Population Statistics: 1. National Data*, p. 12.

4. *Estimates of Future Population by States* (Washington: National Resources Committee, 1934). The thirteen southern states include Oklahoma and Kentucky, but not West Virginia, Maryland, and Delaware.

5. *Negroes in the United States 1920–1932*, pp. 9, 10. The 92 per cent is based on 1860 figures. "South" is used as in the federal census.

Page 11. 6. *Ibid.*, appendix, pp. 683–845; also pp. 9, 25.

7. *Ibid.*, p. 53.

8. *Ibid.*, p. 7. 1890 figures from *Thirteenth Census of the United States, 1910. Population*, Vol. I, p. 184.

9. *Negroes in the United States 1920–1932*, pp. 54, 55.

10. *Ibid.*, p. 89.

Page 12. 11. *Ibid.*, p. 88.

12. *Ibid.*, p. 87. Median age of Negroes has increased from 17.3 in 1850 to 23.4 in 1930.

13. *Ibid.*, p. 91.

II. LIFE AND DEATH

Page 16. "It is not difficult . . ."
Louis I. Dublin and Alfred J. Lotka, *Twenty-Five Years of Health Progress* (New York: Metropolitan Life Insurance Co., 1937), pp. 19–20.

Page 17. The Days of Their Youth
Twenty-Five Years of Health Progress, pp. 38–39. These data are for colored youth but most of them are Negroes.

Page 18. 1. *Twenty-Five Years of Health Progress*, pp. 88, 126, 256, 294, 325. See also Mary Gover, "Trend of Mortality among Southern Negroes Since 1920," *Journal of Negro Education*, VI (July 1937), 280.

2. Bureau of the Census Press Release, No. 48, April 20, 1938, Washington, D. C.

3. *Negroes in the United States 1920–1932* (Washington: U. S. Bureau of the Census, 1935), p. 1.

4. *Problems of a Changing Population* (Washington: National Resources Committee, 1938), p. 134.

5. *Twenty-Five Years of Health Progress*, p. 19.

Page 19. 6. Dorothy F. Holland and George St. J. Perrott, "Health of the Negro," *Milbank Memorial Fund Quarterly Bulletin* (January 1938), pp. 33–34.

7. Allon Peebles, *A Survey of Statistical Data on Medical Facilities in the United States* (Washington: Committee on the Cost of Medical Care, 1929), Pub. No. 3, pp. 30, 68, 90. See also *Negroes in the United States 1920–1932*, p. 292.

8. *Twenty-Five Years of Health Progress*, pp. 347–48.

Page 20. 9. *Ibid.*, p. 20.

10. *Ibid.*, p. 122.

11. *Ibid.*, p. 254.

12. *Ibid.*, pp. 82, 86, 99.

13. *Ibid.*, pp. 371, 373.

Page 21. Tuberculosis and Youth
Twenty-Five Years of Health Progress, p. 82. The term "colored" means essentially Negro.

Page 22. 14. *Ibid.*, pp. 369–70.

15. *Ibid.*, pp. 517–18.

16. *Ibid.*, pp. 173–75.

17. *Ibid.*, pp. 409, 411.

18. *Ibid.*, p. 458.

19. *Ibid.*, pp. 38–39.

III. NO PLACE LIKE HOME

Page 27. "Colored male policyholders . . ."
Louis I. Dublin and Alfred J. Lotka, *Twenty-Five Years of Health Progress* (New York: Metropolitan Life Insurance Co., 1937), p. 488.

"If by subterfuge . . ."
E. B. Reuter, *The American Race Problem* (New York: Thomas Y. Crowell, rev. ed. 1938), p. 223.

Page 28. Low-cost housing—
U. S. Housing Authority, Washington, D. C. One in a hundred based on an estimate of 4,000,000 Negro families.

Page 29. Your Family and Mine
Negroes in the United States 1920–1932 (Washington: U. S. Bureau of the Census, 1935), Table 22, p. 259.

Page 30. 1. *Negroes in the United States 1920–1932*, p. 253.

2. *Negro Year Book 1937–38*, Monroe N. Work, editor (Tuskegee, Alabama: Negro Year Book Publishing Co., 1939), p. 1. Per capita wealth based on 11,891,000 Negroes of 1930.

3, 4. *Negroes in the United States 1920–1932*, p. 147.

Page 31. 5, 6. *Ibid.*, p. 255.

7. *Ibid.*, pp. 256, 259.

8. *Ibid.*, p. 255.

9. Data furnished by Robert C. Weaver, director of racial relations, U. S. Housing Authority, Washington, D. C.

IV. LITERACY AND LEARNING

Page 35. Illiteracy—
Negroes in the United States 1920–1932 (Washington: U. S. Bureau of the Census, 1935), p. 230. For 1865 Bond gives "No less than 93 per cent"; Caliver gives 95 per cent. See H. M. Bond, *Education of the Negro in the American Social Order* (New York: Prentice-Hall, Inc., 1934), pp. 179–80; and Ambrose Caliver, *Availability of Education to Negroes in Rural Communities* (Washington: U. S. Office of Education), Bulletin, 1935, No. 12, p. 9. For the figure 37 per cent see Bond, p. 225.
Income—
Report on Economic Conditions of the South (Washington: National Emergency Council, 1938), p. 21.

Page 36. $44.31 and $12.57—
Ambrose Caliver, *Fundamentals in the Education of Negroes* (Washington: U. S. Office of Education), Bulletin, 1935, No. 6, p. 80.
"By comparison with . . ."
H. M. Bond, "Education in the South," *The Journal of Educational Sociology,* XII (January 1939), 273.

Page 37. Education Free but Not Equal
Doxey A. Wilkerson, *Special Problems of Negro Education* (Washington: Advisory Committee on Education, 1939), p. 50.

Page 38. Land-grant colleges—
Land-Grant Colleges and Universities (Washington: U. S. Office of Education), Circular 176 for year ending June 30, 1938, pp. 7, 15, 21.
"In the present period . . ."
Charles S. Johnson, *A Preface to Racial Understanding* New York: Friendship Press, 1936), p. 79.
1. *Negroes in the United States 1920–1932* (Washington: U. S. Bureau of the Census, 1935), p. 236.

Page 39. 2. *Ibid.,* pp. 238, 251.
3. WPA Mimeographed Compilation, Doc. No. 13990, p. 11.
4. *Negroes in the United States 1920–1932,* p. 231, for 1890 figures. The 1936 estimate of 11.4 per cent is the 1930 figure of 16.3 per cent diminished by 30 per cent.
5. Data from office of Director of Negro Affairs, NYA, Washington, D. C.
6. *Report of the Committee* (Washington: Advisory Committee on Education, 1938), p. 11.

Page 40. 7. *Biennial Survey of Education 1934–36* (Washington: U. S. Office of Education), Chap. II, "Statistics of State School Systems," pp. 14, 48.
8. Ambrose Caliver, *Availability of Education to Negroes in Rural Communities,* Bulletin, 1935, No. 12, pp. 10, 45.

9. *Fifteenth Census of the United States, 1930. Population.* Vol. III (Washington: U. S. Bureau of the Census), Parts I and II, Table 6.

10. Ambrose Caliver, *Vocational Education and Guidance of Negroes* (Washington: U. S. Office of Education), Bulletin, 1937, No. 38, p. 17.

11. *Ibid.,* p. 18.

12. *General Recommendations on Vocational Education and Guidance in New York City* (New York: Vocational Survey Commission of New York City, 1931).

Page 41. 13. NYA Press Release, Serial No. 13982, Washington, D. C.

14. Ambrose Caliver, *Statistics of the Education of Negroes* (Washington: U. S. Office of Education, 1936), p. 11.

15. Charles S. Johnson, *The Negro College Graduate* (Chapel Hill, N. C.: University of North Carolina Press, 1938), pp. 22–23.

V. LIVING OFF THE SOIL

Page 45. Number of tenants—
Negroes in the United States 1920–1932 (Washington: U. S. Bureau of the Census, 1935), p. 577.
Farm wage scale—
Negro Year Book 1937–38, Monroe N. Work, editor (Tuskegee, Alabama: Negro Year Book Publishing Co., 1939), pp. 32–33.

Page 46. 1. *Negroes in the United States 1920–1932,* p. 289.

2. *Problems of a Changing Population* (Washington: National Resources Committee, 1938), p. 76.

3. *Negroes in the United States 1920–1932,* p. 290.

Page 47. 4. *Ibid.,* p. 569.

5. *Ibid.,* p. 577.

6. *Ibid.,* p. 577. See also *Negro Population 1790–1915* (Washington: U. S. Bureau of the Census, 1918), p. 553.

For the 1935 figure see *U. S. Census of Agriculture: 1935* (Washington: U. S. Bureau of the Census, 1936), Vol. III, p. 108.

7. *U. S. Census of Agriculture: 1935*, Vol. I, p. xvi. "Colored" means all non-whites excluding Mexicans and Hindus.

8. *Negroes in the United States 1920–1932*, p. 570.

9. *Problems of a Changing Population*, p. 60.

Page 48. 10. E. A. Schuler, *Social Status and Farm Tenure* (Washington: Works Progress Administration), Study No. IV, pp. 47, 54, 251. Schuler sampled in all about 835 Negro farm families but he obtained certain data from one in five, or 167 families.

11. U. S. Bureau of Home Economics Press Release, Serial No. 1157-38, Feb. 17, 1938, Washington, D. C.

VI. RACIAL COMPETITION FOR JOBS

Page 53. When the Manna Faileth
Final Report on Total and Partial Unemployment (Washington: Census of Partial Employment, Unemployment, and Occupations, 1938), Vol. IV, p. 39.

Page 54. 1. *Negroes in the United States 1920–1932* (Washington: U. S. Bureau of the Census, 1935), p. 288.

2. *Ibid.*, p. 288.

3. *Ibid.*, p. 290.

Page 55. 4. *Report on Economic Conditions of the South* (Washington: National Emergency Council, 1938), p. 20.

5, 6, 7. *5,000,000 Jobs; the Negro at Work in the United States* (New York: National Urban League, 1933), The Color Line Series, No. 2, pp. 12–20.

8. *Final Report on Total and Partial Unemployment*, Vol. IV, pp. 38–39. The percentages for colored youth, 95 per cent of whom were Negro, are probably quite accurate for the latter group.

Page 56. 9. Howard Bell, *Youth Tell Their Story* (Washington: American Council on Education, 1938), pp. 112, 109, 120.

Page 57. 10. *Urban Youth, Their Characteristics and Economic Problems* (Washington: Works Progress Administration, 1939), Division of Research, Study No. 24, p. 45.
11. Joseph J. Lister and E. L. Kirkpatrick, *Rural Youth Speak* (Washington: American Youth Commission, 1939), p. 37. (Mimeographed)

VII. THE NEGRO PROFESSIONAL

Page 61. Occupations—
Alba Edwards, *A Social-Economic Grouping of the Gainful Workers of the United States, 1930.* (Washington: U. S. Bureau of the Census, 1938), p. 13.

Payrolls—
Negroes in the United States 1920–1932 (Washington: U. S. Bureau of the Census, 1935), p. 498, and *Census of Business: 1935. Retail Distribution* (Washington: U. S. Bureau of the Census, 1937), "U. S. Summary" Vol. I, Part I, p. 42.

Retail sales—
Negroes in the United States 1920–1932, p. xiv, and *Census of Business: 1935. Retail Distribution*, "U. S. Summary," Vol. I, Part I, p. 42.

Page 62. Incomes—
Family Income in Chicago, 1935–36 (Washington: U. S. Bureau of Labor Statistics), Bulletin No. 642, Vol. I, p. 24.

Clergymen—
Negroes in the United States 1920–1932, p. 292. *Fifteenth Census of the United States, 1930. Population: General Report on Occupations*, Vol. V (Washington: U. S. Bureau of the Census), p. 574.

Page 63. The Work Pattern
Alba Edwards, *A Social-Economic Grouping of the Gainful Workers of the United States, 1930*, pp. 28, 40.

130

Page 64. 1. *Census of Business: 1935, Service Establishments* (Washington: U. S. Bureau of the Census, 1936), "U. S. Summary," Vol. I, pp. 16–17.

2. *Census of Business: 1935, Retail Distribution,* "U. S. Summary," Vol. I, Part 1, p. 42.

3. *Negro Year Book 1936–37,* Monroe N. Work, editor (Tuskegee, Alabama: Negro Year Book Publishing Co., 1938), pp. 92–93. Authorities disagree as to the exact number of Negro banks.

4. *A Social-Economic Grouping of the Gainful Workers of the United States, 1930,* p. 60.

5. *Ibid.,* pp. 10, 13.

Page 65. 6. *Ibid.,* pp. 46–47.

VIII. RELIEF AND RECOVERY

Page 69. Relief—

Negro division, WPA, Washington, D. C. See also *Negro Year Book 1937–38,* Monroe N. Work, editor (Tuskegee, Alabama: Negro Year Book Publishing Co., 1938), p. 20.

Page 70. Social Security accounts—

Social Security Board, Inquiry Section, Washington, D. C.

Page 71. 1. Estimates supplied by Racial Relations Office, Federal Works Agency.

2. W. G. Daniel and C. L. Miller, "Participation of the Negro in the National Youth Administration Program," *Journal of Negro Education,* VII (July 1938), 361.

3. Figures supplied by Granville Dickey, CCC, Washington, D. C.

Page 72. 4. *Statistics of Youth on Relief* (Washington: Works Progress Administration, Jan. 6, 1936), Division of Social Research, Research Bulletin, Series I, No. 16, pp. 24–25.

5. NYA Press Release, Serial No. 13982, Washington, D. C.

6. Quotation from Social Security Board, Inquiry Section, Washington, D. C.

7. NYA Press Release, Serial No. 13982, Washington, D. C.

IX. LEISURE AND PLAY

Page 77. 1. Doxey A. Wilkerson, *Special Problems of Negro Education* (Washington: Advisory Committee on Education, 1939), p. 148.
2. *Ibid.*, p. 150.

Page 78. 3. *Ibid.*, p. 150.
4. Faith M. Williams and Alice C. Hansen, *Money Disbursements of Wage Earners and Clerical Workers in the North Atlantic Region*, 1931–36 (Washington: U. S. Bureau of Labor Statistics, 1939), Bulletin No. 637, pp. 142–43.
5. *Social Work Year Book, 1935*, F. S. Hall and M. B. Ellis, editors (New York: Russell Sage Foundation, 1936), p. 295.
6. Facts supplied by Ernest T. Atwell, National Recreation Association, New York City.

Page 79. 7, 8. Facts supplied by Ernest T. Atwell, National Recreation Association, New York City.

X. LET US PRAY

Page 84. "Bishops without a diocese . . ."
Ira DeA. Reid, "Let Us Prey," *Opportunity, Journal of Negro Life*, IV (September 1926), 277.

Page 85. Let Us Pray
Negroes in the United States 1920–1932 (Washington: U. S. Bureau of the Census, 1935), p. 531.

Page 86. 1. C. Luther Fry, *The U. S. Looks at Its Churches* (New York: Institute of Social and Religious Research, 1930), p. 63.
2. *Negroes in the United States, 1920–1932*, p. 530.
3. *Ibid.*, pp. 530–32.

Page 87. 4. Carter G. Woodson, *The History of the Negro Church* (Washington: Associated Publishers, 1921), p. 280 ff.
5. *Negroes in the United States 1920–1932*, p. 532.

6. *The U. S. Looks at Its Churches,* pp. 22–23.

7. *Ibid.,* p. 94.

8. *Ibid.,* p. 32.

9. E. B. Reuter, *The American Race Problem* (New York: Thomas Y. Crowell, rev. ed. 1938), p. 318.

XI. THE EVIL MEN DO

Page 92. Criminal patterns—
Clifford R. Shaw and Maurice E. Moore, *The Natural History of a Delinquent Career* (Chicago: University of Chicago Press, 1931).

1. *County and City Jails, 1933* (Washington: U. S. Bureau of the Census, 1935), p. 15.

2. *Federal Offenders, 1936–37* (Washington: U. S. Bureau of Prisons, 1937), p. 208.

Page 93. The Evil Men Do
County and City Jails, 1933, p. 15.

Page 94. 3. *Uniform Crime Reports* (Washington: U. S. Bureau of Investigation, 1938), Vol. IX, No. 4, p. 177.

4. Louis I. Dublin and Alfred J. Lotka, *Twenty-Five Years of Health Progress* (New York: Metropolitan Life Insurance Co., 1937), p. 421.

5. *Ibid.,* pp. 157–58.

6. *Negro Year Book 1937–38,* Monroe N. Work, editor (Tuskegee, Alabama: Negro Year Book Publishing Co., 1938), p. 157.

7. *Ibid.,* p. 426.

Page 95. 8. *Ibid.,* p. 158.

XII. THE LAW

Page 101. The Decline of Lynching
Negro Year Book 1937–38, Monroe N. Work, editor (Tuskegee, Alabama: Negro Year Book Publishing Co., 1939), pp. 156–57.

Page 102. 1. *Black Justice* (New York: American Civil Liberties Union, 1938), p. 4.

2. *Ibid.*, p. 4.

3. *Ibid.*, pp. 4, 14, and Doxey A. Wilkerson, *Special Problems of Negro Education* (Washington: Advisory Committee on Education, 1939), p. xv.

4. *Negro Year Book 1937–38*, p. 144.

Page 103. 5. *Negro Year Book 1931–32*, pp. 204, 140–41

6. *Negro Year Book 1937–38*, pp. 158–59.

7. Walter Wilson, *Forced Labor in the United States* (New York: International Publishers, 1933), p. 93. (*Memphis Press Scimitar*, April 18, 1931, given as reference).

Page 104. 8. *Ibid.*, p. 94.

9. *Ibid.*, pp. 96–97.

XIII. PLANNING FOR SURVIVORS

Page 107. "It is, perhaps . . ."
Charles S. Johnson, *A Preface to Racial Understanding* (New York: Friendship Press, 1936), p. 162.

Page 109. Philanthropy Lends a Hand
Eduard C. Lindeman, *Wealth and Culture* (New York: Harcourt, Brace and Co., 1935), appendix, pp. 67–135.

COVER PHOTOGRAPH: LIFE Magazine

134

THE AMERICAN COUNCIL ON EDUCATION
GEORGE F. ZOOK, *President*

The American Council on Education is a *council* of national educational associations; organizations having related interests; approved universities and colleges, technological schools, and private secondary schools; state departments of education; and city school systems. It is a center of cooperation and coordination whose influence has been apparent in the shaping of American educational policies as well as in the formulation of American educational practices during the past twenty years. Many leaders in American education and public life serve on the commissions and committees through which the Council operates.

Established by the Council in 1935, the American Youth Commission consists of the persons whose names appear on a front page of this publication. It operates through a staff under the supervision and control of a director responsible to the Commission.